Citizenship Social Work
with Older People

Also by Malcolm Payne

Humanistic Social Work: Core Principles in Practice (2011)

Social Work in End-of-Life and Palliative Care (with Margaret Reith, 2009)

What Is Professional Social Work? (second edition, 2006)

Modern Social Work Theory (third edition, 2005)

Teamwork in Multiprofessional Care (2000)

Citizenship Social Work with Older People

Malcolm Payne

LYCEUM
BOOKS, INC.

Chicago, Illinois

Published by

LYCEUM BOOKS, INC.
5758 S. Blackstone Avenue
Chicago, Illinois 60637
773-643-1903 fax
773-643-1902 phone
lyceum@lyceumbooks.com
www.lyceumbooks.com

This book is published by arrangement with Opole University. All sales in Poland or in the Polish language are handled by Opole University.

6 5 4 3 2 1   11 12 13 14

ISBN 978-1-935871-08-8

Cover image © Volodymyrkrasyuk—Dreamstime.com

Printed in the United States of America.

Library of Congress Cataloging-in-Publication Data

Payne, Malcolm, 1947–
    Citizenship social work with older people / Malcolm Payne.
       p. cm.
    Includes bibliographical references and index.
    ISBN 978-1-935871-08-8 (pbk. : alk. paper)
  1. Social work with older people. 2. Older people—Services for. 3. Older people—Social conditions. I. Title.
    HV1451.P39   2012
    362.6—dc23
                                                                2011018024

Contents

Boxes

Introduction

AIMS

I recently went to an uncle's diamond wedding (sixtieth) anniversary party and sat at a table next to the widow of one of his work friends, who was herself in her eighties. We talked about computers and the Internet, and she proclaimed herself a "silver surfer." "It's so exciting," she said. "There are so many things you can learn about. Sometimes I stay up half the night on the Internet." Her exploration of the world through her computer was giving her a new interest and commitment in life. In writing this book, I want to encourage social work practice to empower that kind of enthusiasm for life and the world among the older people with whom we work.

My main aim in this book is to develop from existing social work practice ideas a citizenship social work with older people. Citizenship social work starts from the idea that older people are equal as citizens of any society, any state, any community, any family; that citizenship confers rights to participation in and responsibilities for older people and everyone else within those social relationships. I argue that we do not always accord older people those rights in the way we think and the way we act. I use "pause and reflect" sections in this book to enable you to think through your own feelings and views on the topics covered.

PAUSE AND REFLECT: Excluding Older People

Think about your own attitudes to older people: are there ways in which you do not quite think of them as equal citizens?

Some Suggestions
Some people assume that they are not as important as younger people because they are not as in touch with current ideas; they have retired, so they are not making a productive contribution to society; they've lived the main part of their life, so they are not as important as younger people who need education and development for the future; they need care, so they are a drain on family, community, and state resources; they have old-fashioned ideas about behavior; they are irritating and slow.

Are you sure you have not thought at least one of these things sometimes about an older person? If you have, and a lot of people do think in these ways at least sometimes, they are at risk of excluding older people from equal citizenship. My greatest concern is the feeling that they are no longer productive—they have had their lives, so they matter less. Down that line of thinking lies ideas such as perhaps it is less important to treat them when they become ill, that perhaps we should help them to commit suicide if they want to so they are not a burden to society.

These negative thoughts about older people come from a human and social capital perspective on social relations. It says we all have a responsibility to contribute our skills and activity to society, to build society, to make it stronger. Behind this lies an economic view that the main objectives of our life are the development of society and economic growth. Without growth and development, there will be social and economic decline and stagnation.

Social work can never accept such a view. Everyone makes a contribution to the solidarity of society. We need all kinds of people to interact with to experience our own humanity and the humanity of other people. We all need to have the chance to care for our sister and brother human beings. Human cultural and social achievement can come from everyone, everywhere. Social work aims to enable social relationships in all societies to achieve that quality of human interaction; without it, we can ultimately have no quality of life.

In this book, I emphasize finding out for yourself about older people in your society and thinking through creatively and critically how you can best practice. To be creative and critical, we need to practice the skills; doing it as we learn about important topics is a good way of doing so. While I draw on my own knowledge and experience as I write, I am suggesting that the right approach to learning social work is to get out and explore the possibilities. As my uncle's silver surfer friend discovered, there's a world of excitement and interest to be found on the Internet and through personal experience, and it's a do-it-yourself exploration that brings dividends that will fit in with your personal way of working and the personal and individual needs of your clients.

Writing this book for Polish and U.S. publishers comes from working with students of social work and social pedagogy in Opole University in southern Poland over the past few years and having the chance to visit many countries, including the U.S., to see and teach about practice. This book tries to make ideas available from a wide range of sources, as well as my own experience and UK knowledge base. As I write about my experience and knowledge, I have constantly tested it with the question: how can we understand that so that it is relevant in many different settings and cultures?

To make this book more accessible to a wide range of people in the social professions across the world, I have particularly emphasized resources that are available on the Internet. Of course, I have drawn on books and articles in the usual way, but I have made a special effort to use and recommend Internet resources that are freely accessible anywhere. This enables people to look at the creativity so that they can translate to their own practice what is happening across the world.

THE PLAN OF THE BOOK

The first three chapters of the book provide social context for practice with older people. Chapter 1 looks at aging and the experience of older people, chapter 2 at the integration of services so that they experience help as holistic, and chapter 3 at the range of social provision for older people.

The next four chapters focus on social work practice. Chapter 4 examines social work skills needed for practice with older people, chapter 5 at critical practice, chapter 6 at creative practice, and chapter 7 on group and macro practice.

The final chapter looks at issues that may lead to older people being socially excluded from citizenship and how social workers might respond to this.

Contact me through the publishers or through my blog: http://blogs .stchristophers.org.uk/one.

I have included case examples throughout the text, drawn from a wide range of sources, including my practice experience and information from colleagues and students. Where necessary, I have changed personal information that might identify people to preserve their privacy.

Exploring Aging and Older People's Lives

AIMS

Are grandparents as important in a family or community as children? Is caring for them when they need it just as important? If so, we are in solidarity with the older people around us as well as the young. They are citizens in the community traveling along the road through life. That is the principle that lies behind this book.

The first three chapters focus on broader issues about the place of older people and services provided for them in the societies in which they live. Successful social work practice involves individualizing the person you are working with, while at the same time thinking about broader social relationships between younger and older people and between older people as individuals and a wider society in which older people are a significant social group.

The main aim of this first chapter is to introduce general ideas and information about the aging process and social impact of growing older to help social work practitioners understand the experience of the older people who are their clients.

After working through this chapter, readers should have:

- Considered the meaning of a citizenship approach to practice with older people in their social context
- Examined the practice implications of views, assumptions, and theories about aging and the social life of older people, including readers' own views and assumptions
- Considered the changing social and economic settlement within which policy and practice with older people is framed
- Assessed the implications for policy and practice of biomedical understanding of aging

CITIZENSHIP SOCIAL WORK: HELPING CITIZENS TO AGE

We all grow old. We experience physical changes as we age, but also we age in a social place; we age within the social relationships and context that have formed our lives. Each person fashions their old age as part of a life. Every society and each part of any society constructs its views of human aging, and in doing so both constricts and facilitates ways to respond to it. The aim of social work with older people is to assist people in living with their aging and to empower societies to engage with aging among other aspects of life.

A citizenship social work starts from two-sided analysis of individual and social experiences of aging. So therefore does this book and this chapter. But citizenship social work does not neglect the impact of physical aging on individuals, families, communities, societies, or their quality of life. Citizenship social work proposes that social workers have a humanistic duty in their practice to facilitate people's human capacity, living in social groups and accepting collective responsibility for each other, to seek their own personal growth toward a good quality of life and personal and collective freedom for themselves and others (Payne, 2011). Citizenship is two-way: citizens participate and societies accept responsibility for the quality of the lives that citizens live. Because aging is universal, and because citizenship invokes participation in the society in which citizens live, social work based on citizenship treats all human beings as equal in their right to justice and respect for their personal dignity, as internationally adopted charters of human rights propose (Payne, 2011). Human rights ideas say that the law, the state, and professions such as social work must sustain those values in their policy and practice.

Social provision and social work often focus on people who either have problems in society or are problems to society. Despite this, older people are not some different, distant, and problematic social group; old age is the future for us all. Achieving justice, human rights, and dignity for older people is not a distant ideal but an ever-present social duty that we owe to people who share the same humanity and citizenship as ourselves. Social change, policy developments, and professional practices in social work with older people therefore speak about how we ourselves expect and want to be: equal, respected, and dignified citizens.

Two-way citizenship means that social provision and social work have a positive focus: facilitating and empowering effective social responses to the issues that societies face. Older people offer us an opportunity to empower solidarity in our society as we work to identify ways in which aging requires extra help to enable their equality in respect and dignity as citizens to be expressed in the quality of their lives and the opportunities they have to fulfill their human potential.

ATTITUDES TO AGING

Because these social values are so important, the introduction asked you to pause and reflect on your attitudes to older people. Going further, what are your attitudes to aging? When we are evaluating policy and practice, we need to keep a constant self-check to make sure we are treating older people as part of the same humanity and citizenship as younger people. Our practice and our thoughts should never be excluding and disrespectful.

PAUSE AND REFLECT: Experiences of and Attitudes to Growing Older

What is your age? What is the best age to be? When are you at your peak? You are older than you were—what difference has aging meant to you? If you are a student or worker, are you the same age as people in your class or job level? Does age define your grade in school, college, or work? Do you mix more with older people at work than you did in school? Compare yourself with your parents and your grandparents. They are older than you—in what ways does that make them different from you? In what ways do your parents differ from your grandparents because of age differences?

Some Suggestions

You might have expressed your age as a number: twenty-four, forty-eight, or fifty-nine; or as a range: your twenties or forties; or as a life stage: student, young, or middle-aged. The range or life stage might have carried implications for you and others. You might think that the best age is when your body is young, at its physical peak. Then, at different ages, we live our life in different ways, and this leads to different relationships between the ages. For example, students are likely to live in groups of young people, separately from older people. Older people that they meet might be teachers or friends of their parents. Some ages define where you are in school or a university course, and you mainly mix with people in your year of development. In other stages of life and in families, you mix with people from every age. Perhaps, comparing yourself with parents or grandparents, you thought that the older age groups were less in touch with modern technology, social development, and language. They have mobile phones but use them less frequently, are not so good at sending text messages, and do not use the camera features because they prefer a separate single-purpose camera. Your grandparents still send written letters to people, perhaps. The older age groups are also slightly more formal in how they greet you, how they dress, and how they use less up-to-date language.

We can explore different generations' experiences by looking at a history of events and comparing the ages of different birth cohorts when they experienced them. People in any society or nation experience the same events but, depending on their age when the event occurs, at different stages of their lives. For example, the fall of the Berlin Wall in 1989, leading to economic and social transition in many Eastern European countries, will have been experienced differently in Poland and the U.S. and differently again by different age groups. In Poland, people born in 1920 had a childhood in the period of Polish independence, adult experience of World War II, which was particularly devastating in Poland, and much of their later adult lifetime spent under the communist regime. Someone born in Poland in 1948 spent his or her childhood and young adulthood under the communist regime, and was in middle age when the transition started. Someone born in 1989 would not remember the communist period, but his or her childhood would have been affected by the economic and social dislocation and development arising from the transition. Many people of all ages in Poland will have ambivalent feelings about these events. Most people in the U.S. will barely be aware of important events in Poland, may see the transition as a victory for their economic system and lifestyle, and may be unaware of the difficulties of the transition period.

PAUSE AND REFLECT: Comparing Generations

Box 1.1 is drawn from a similar table in Rees Jones et al. (2008, pp. 23–24). You could ask people at different ages about their experience of events that you have chosen from an account of modern history in your country, ask them to select events that were significant to them, and try these out on other people.

Box 1.1 Experience of Life Events by Different Age Cohorts

Category of event	Year	Event	Birth cohort		
			1935	1948	1990
Economic and political change	1945	End of World War II	10		
	1991	Soviet Union dismantled	56	43	1
	2001	9/11 attack on World Trade Center in New York	66	53	11
Cultural events	1948	Transistor radio invented	13	0	
	1961	Oral contraception launched	26	13	
	1991	World Wide Web	56	43	1

Source: developed from Rees Jones et al. (2008)

Some Suggestions

Examining the different experience of age cohorts often draws attention to some of the reasons for widely varying attitudes between the generations. It also draws attention to personal experience: someone who was there or went through a social change is much more conscious of the practical and personal consequences of what happened than someone who only heard or read about it.

The aim of this reflection is to raise awareness of the different perceptions of events in different age cohorts. A practitioner needs to be aware of the difference between their own life experiences and that of their clients, as well as differences between their clients' experiences and those of the clients' informal caregivers and family members they are in contact with.

SOCIAL THEORIES OF AGING

Main Types of Aging Theories

Aging is not just a biological process, therefore, because how we deal with it is affected by expectations and ideas about aging in our society. Social theories of aging offer organized models of the aging process and its social consequences. Estes and Associates (2001) divide them into two groups:

- Gerontological theories organize social understandings of aging as a biological process that has social effects. Social construction ideas and structural perspectives develop these theories.
- Critical analyses of social ideas of aging, such as conflict theories, ideas about social change, and concerns about systemic crises in provision of services policy for older people offer a critique of gerontological ideas.

In addition to these social theories:

- Biological or medical approaches to aging focus mainly on physical changes associated with older age groups.

Gerontological theories focus on the social consequences of biological aging for older people and the families, communities, and society around them. They therefore often take for granted the assumption that obvious physical changes as people age are an important factor in living as an older person. Such ideas may build on everyday social observations about aging and make sense of them. The problem is that this could lead us to accept that the body is at its best when we are young, so aging is negative, a deterioration from our peak. Or we might think that it is important to help children develop, because they are the future, so we fail to look for ways of making a positive difference in the lives of older people. Critical theories are helpful because the discourse between them and our taken-for-granted assumptions about aging alerts us to keep our minds open about appropriate aims for policy and practice.

Disengagement, Continuity, and Activity

An important, but now seriously questioned, gerontological theory of aging refers to disengagement. The assumption that society makes less use of older people and that they are less use to society is a powerful one. Early explanations about the sociology of aging therefore focused on how some older people progressively disengage from their lifestyle in adulthood. For example, most people retire from working, and, in some countries, there are formal retiring ages, at which we have a party, get a gift, and receive our pension. Older people may follow this up and reduce commitments to organized social activity and withdraw from active roles in child care and family life. Their social life reduces, and they spend more time at home doing relatively passive activities. As their physical and perhaps mental frailty increases, their capacity to do practical tasks to maintain their house and garden reduces, and they may become housebound or bedbound.

While this may be true for some people in some societies, many people do not fit this pattern or only disengage for a short period prior to a final illness at the end of their lives. Moreover, it is clearly not a universal explanation of the social process of aging because in many societies (for example, in developing countries), older people have to continue working for as long as possible in order to have an income. They may also live their whole lives within an extended family, active in family life, even if frailty eventually reduces their external connections.

Competing gerontological ideas in contrast focus on the level and extent of older people's activity and its continuity of their interests and activities with their previous life. Such theories seek to understand how older people can create for themselves a successful and productive aging process. Three factors are important:

- Retaining good health accompanied by a low probability of ill health, which allows people to plan for the future with confidence
- Good mental and physical capacities, which allow people to make choices about their lifestyle
- Active engagement with past life and in developing new interests and contacts

Case Example: Two Mothers

My mother and my wife's mother were of the generation that lived as adults through the Second World War and, after marriage in the 1940s, became full-time mothers, also keeping house for their families.

My mother's life after my father died in his mid-fifties is an example of disengagement. She returned to work for a few years in clerical jobs, retiring at sixty, the state pension age. For a few years, she continued membership of local organizations, accepting a committee role in one as she had more time than when she worked. She kept up family links, visiting her sisters in other parts of town and my family in other parts of the country. She went on a seaside holiday annually, staying at a hotel on her own in a resort well-known for catering to older people.

However, as she approached seventy years, she gradually withdrew from these activities, telling me that they now held no interest for her. She continued to watch television most evenings and to read novels borrowed from the local library. A lifelong physical disability increasingly affected her, and she had a fall in a local shop, after which she refused to go out and moved her bed from the upper floor of the family house to a downstairs room. She complained that her sisters' homes were noisy and disorganized and ceased visiting them, and also stopped visiting my family as my two young sons became more boisterous; instead we visited her for shorter trips. Paid caregivers from local social services bought her shopping, cooked meals, and did practical tasks around the home, neglecting her once much-loved garden; they also bought cheap novels from local shops to replace her library visits. She refused, except in one emergency, to be picked up by car and taken out or to family visits and events. A next-door neighbor, when she was in town, visited twice a day. My mother would only answer the telephone if we called at a planned time; her younger sister and I had set weekly times to call. For security reasons, she would not answer the door to visitors, unless they had planned the visit in advance—it was impossible to drop in. This pattern went on for eleven years, until her physical condition deteriorated. She fell several times and was admitted to hospital twice for a few days, being rehabilitated on the first occasion by a physiotherapist. She eventually died of a lung infection during the second hospital admission.

My wife's mother also lost her husband early but found work as a non-qualified social work assistant. Her aging is an example of activity and continuity. Too late in life to start social work training and develop a career, she undertook counseling training and set up a private practice as a counselor, which she continued after retirement age, improving her retirement income. She joined the committees of counseling professional bodies and provided supervision to a number of colleagues. In her fifties, she experienced a bout of cancer, but after treatment went into remission and, although she had subsequent physical problems, continued to live at home. She started an interest in gardening, maintaining a large garden. Her three children and six grandchildren stayed regularly, and she continued to visit long-standing friends and attend family events in different parts of the country. For the first time in her life, accompanied by one of her children or a friend, she began to travel abroad regularly. She died in her mid-seventies, being admitted to hospital with a recurrence of cancer less than two weeks after her last counseling appointment and died six weeks later.

Practice and Policy Implications

We saw above that, as they age, people experience a wide range of social change. We can understand what has happened to the present generation of older people in developed countries in a variety of different ways:

- From being physically and socially active participants in a range of activities to experiencing declining physical capacity
- From being workers to being retired
- From being passive recipients of official services to being active consumers of goods and services (Rees Jones et al., 2008)

The last two might not be true of older people in less-developed countries. However, none of these changes necessarily involves disengagement from a previous life. Citizenship implies that a society maintains social responsibility for people whatever their style of life as they age and that older people retain the right and duty of participation in that society. Therefore, practitioners and policymakers need to practice and plan services in ways that assume a wide range of reactions to these common social changes. Even where disengagement does occur, or physical frailty increases, it may be possible for practitioners to change someone's assumptions so that they regain continuity and activity in their lives.

The Life Course and Control of the Aging Process

Other gerontological theories of aging try to incorporate this flexibility because, while they identify patterns in the aging process, they also emphasize different behavioral and social reactions to those patterns.

Life course theories of aging see people as going through a number of stages of their lives, each stage being characterized by particular experiences shared by many in that phase of life. Erikson's (1977) life cycle ideas, mainly focused on younger ages, saw people going through a series of similar stages that they had to negotiate successfully. Each phase in the life course is a preparation for later stages. This leads to people developing resilience and skill at earlier stages that will facilitate successful negotiation of later stages of the life course. People experience transitions to the next stage. Social factors in the environment affect how individuals react to physical changes as they age and to these transitions. Such factors include:

- Social support through interpersonal relationships
- Coping skills and mechanisms that an older person possesses
- Their degree of control over events that affect them
- Their self-efficacy, that is, their self-confidence that they either have or can build the capacity to deal with adverse events
- Cognitive and behavioral aspects of life, for example, whether an older person has the intellectual and creative skills to analyze and respond to events and can manage emotional reactions such as anger, anxiety, depression, or distress appropriately

Guillemard (2005) divides the life course into three; Koskinen (1994) connected these phases to major changes in the way people are supported financially, as follows:

- Childhood, during which we are maintained by our parents and state support for education, leisure, and personal development
- Adulthood, in which paid employment allows us to maintain ourselves; if we cannot work, social security provides some compensation
- Postretirement, when financial transfers from our adult period and from the rest of the population through various pension and medical supports allow us to retire from employment

Increasingly, the shifts between the three phases are changing, and most people's life courses are more flexible than this analysis assumes. For example, enterprising children with physical skills for sport or in contact with modern technology and popular culture can see ways to make fortunes from early business or sporting success. Adults take sabbaticals during which they travel and concentrate on personal development. Older people continue working, either because of lack of financial support or to maintain a more interesting and better-financed lifestyle. Increasingly, too, people want a better work-life balance in the adult phase. So they work part-time, with reduced income, so that they can enjoy being with their children or pursuing leisure and personal development interests. However, those career breaks or periods of reduced income may make it difficult for people to support themselves in later life from their income in middle adulthood.

One of the problems with life course theory is that it focuses on the period of bearing and bringing up children, so it can exclude older age groups from serious consideration. This stops us from thinking about valuable contributions that older people can make to society.

Practice and Policy Implications

Seeing aging as a process that has continuity with previous stages of life and emphasizing the possibility of actively planning and managing what happens during later life raises important possibilities. It suggests that we should actively seek to prepare people for later life and persuade them to plan for likely contingencies. While doing so, helping people to retain continuity with past activities and relationships and to think about how they will develop new activities, relationships, and contributions to society enables them to avoid becoming unintentionally disengaged and to remain as active citizens. However, their plans need flexibility to deal with unexpected events.

Case Example: Retirement Plans

My uncle Brian's life in his seventies is an example of life course planning going wrong. He and his wife saw his retirement—he was younger than she was but more prone to ill health—as an opportunity to fulfill an ambition to live in another part of the country, close to many of her relatives. It was a rural seaside location, where they had often vacationed. They downsized from their expensive city apartment to a convenient bungalow, releasing money to be invested to increase their pension income. They saw this very much as a positive life change; it was not disengagement because they made plans to recreate a new life that included new activities, and connections with her relatives provided a ready-made social circle. Unfortunately, soon after the move, his wife died from undiagnosed cancer. Because of his ill health, they had organized their affairs so that many of their financial resources were in her name, and he had considerable legal problems for more than a year in getting access to money to live on. Without her, contacts with her family were less easy to maintain; and his eyesight deteriorated, making new contacts and carrying on old pursuits more difficult. Eventually, after admission to hospital for a stomach condition, he did not start eating again and died a few days later.

Social Construction Theories

A criticism of the theories we have so far examined is their focus on individual psychological factors. It is also important to examine social forces and their influence on social change as a way of understanding aging. As we have seen, one generation's experience is different from the previous generation's. Many psychological theories also assume that similar experiences affect all older people, rather than picking up on variability within the same age group, affected by such factors as poverty and social class. Most people's choices in how they live through the aging process are constrained by such social factors.

Social construction theories therefore seek to explore how the physical and social environment has an impact on the experience of aging, and the impact of social relationships and encounters between people as they age influences how people see the aging process. An example of this sort of understanding of aging is recent concern about intergenerational conflict over resources. Willetts (2010) argues that the cohort of baby boomers, people approaching retirement during the period 2011 to 2030, benefited financially and in social mobility from the long period of post–World War II economic growth, while their children have had much less opportunity to accumulate wealth before retirement. He suggests that this may lead to unfairness between the generations, since generous pensions with rules established during successful economic periods must be paid for by later generations whose provision is less generous. The opposite point of view suggests that a better-off parental generation is more able to subsidize younger generations. However, this benefits social groups that are already wealthy enough to subsidize their children and may disadvantage people from lower socioeconomic groups.

Practice and Policy Implications

Some social perspectives on aging suggest that we should examine differential experience of age cohorts and interactions between them. An important policy and practice objective may be to reduce intergenerational conflict. Similarly, it is important for policies to keep pace with economic and demographic change. For example, pensions may become less sustainable economically as life expectancy rises significantly and retirement policies and expectations may need to change.

Critical Theories

Critical theories offer a range of ideas that in various ways question taken-for-granted assumptions that underlie many of these ideas about aging. While social construction ideas raise questions about individualized, psychological explanations about social responses to aging, they still examine relatively small-scale social change. Critical theory incorporates a range of ideas that ask about potential conflicts among interest groups and stakeholders. For example:

- Conflict theory asks: who dominates or benefits from the current socioeconomic system?
- Feminist theory examines how aging accentuates gender divisions. Some stereotypes about aging focus on men's experience. For example, ideas about retirement often emphasize how men lose time and relationships in their lives when they retire, instead of looking at opportunities for men to be reintegrated into family and community relationships alongside and more equally with women.
- Critical theory focuses on how dominant ideas in society are emphasized in cultural assumptions about social structures such as retirement. Industrialized societies often see retirement as a less valuable phase of life than working, but this says that economic outputs of a labor force are important, rather than looking at artistic human achievement, personal and social satisfaction in relationships, and enjoyment of leisure.
- Focusing on discrimination against older people raises questions about ageism that extend beyond individual prejudices. Bytheway (1995) suggests that ageism builds from the assumption that people only have value if they are valued and valuable economically. It extends into cultural perceptions of attractiveness, with the young body being more attractive than older bodies. Older men seek to retain power and money while older women lose much that they had during their working lives in social isolation, domestic responsibility, and family poverty. Dependence on younger people for economic and practical support is regarded as an economic and emotional burden.
- Ideas about the medicalization and commodification of aging criticize common assumptions about older age groups. The critique of medicalization argues that it is inappropriate to see the main problem about aging as rising illness and disability and the main necessity as health and social care services. The commodification critique proposes that services for older people may be understood as being concerned with making society more efficient by reducing the cost of dependence on the working population.
- The critique of privatization and rationalization in policy about aging suggests that the main purpose of social policy about older age groups is economic efficiency and reducing needs and wants, rather than valuing the social contribution made by older people.
- The critique of the view that there is a systemic crisis of or services for older age groups suggests that our social provision should value the

humanity and social contribution of all groups, rather than see ourselves as in crisis because there are too many older people to care for.

Summary: Thinking about Aging

I have argued that it is important for people who are working with older people to think about their clients' experience of aging and to understand some of the processes that are taking place as people age. It is useful to put this in context by considering some of the theories of aging. I suggested that we need to think about personal psychological reactions to aging as well as social forces that may bring change that people and societies must cope with. Practitioners may be particularly affected by ageist ideas focusing on older people's dependence and burden, rather than the positive focus on opportunity offered by citizenship practice.

THE CHANGING SOCIAL SETTLEMENT FOR OLDER PEOPLE

Aging theories point to the importance of social change and its effects on life for older people. The social settlement for older people is changing across the world. That is, until the millennium, most people had settled, accepted expectations at least in developed societies about aging and social provision for older people. But these ideas are changing because of a variety of social pressures. The assumption that there is a settled view of older people is not true across the whole world or for all time and every culture. On the contrary, people's experience of aging has changed markedly over time. Only some, mainly developed, countries have established systems of retirement and pension provision, and some cultures actively value the role of older people as part of multi-generational families. To practice effectively in the social professions with older people, it is important to be aware of these changes and differences and assess the social pressures in the particular society that are relevant to older people as they age.

Demographic Change

One reason that the social settlement is changing is demographic change everywhere, but particularly affecting developed countries. According to the UN Programme on Ageing, the proportion of people aged sixty and over in the world population rose to 10 percent in 2000 and will double by 2050 to 21 percent, meaning that more than one in five people will be an older person. The overall number of older persons will increase more than threefold from 606 million in 2000 to 1.9 billion in 2050. This change affects all nations. In developed countries, the number of people over sixty will increase by almost 70 percent, from

232 million in 2000 to 394 million in 2050; and developing regions will see a fourfold increase, from 375 million in 2000 to 1.5 billion in 2050 (Venne, n.d.).

This demographic change is altering the social settlement around aging because increased numbers of older people raise fears that present assumptions about working life and financing retirement will be increasingly unsustainable. Until the second half of the twentieth century, as people lived longer, they extended their working life. This process has stopped, and people now live a long time after the end of the normal period of working life. As a result, pensions and other financial arrangements to support retirement have increasingly become inadequate. These changes do not just have an impact on older people themselves. They also affect the whole of society because it has to deal with the cultural, practical, and social changes that arise from a greater proportion of the population being older.

However, as we noted when looking at theories of aging, it is important to test social reactions to these changes against the possibility that ageist fears about older people becoming a burden leads us to exaggerate this as an economic and service provision crisis. A recent EU review (Commission of the European Communities, 2009) puts it like this. Most older people in the EU can expect to live healthy and active lives, continuing their former lifestyles and participating actively in social relationships. However, most EU countries are experiencing a trend toward longer lives and lower birth rates. Many EU states are making changes in preparation for the impact of these, mainly in pension and family policy.

Older People's Dependence

The concerns about these changes are the same as those in most other developed countries. A larger population of older people will be practically and economically dependent on a smaller population of working age.

Looking first at practical dependence, why should older people become dependent? Sennett (2003) makes the point that, in private life, dependence creates ties, and psychology and many cultural traditions value interdependence. Liberal political philosophy sees dependence as infantilization and connects independence with the work ethic: if we work to look after ourselves, we contribute to society rather than drawing from it. The concern about dependence among older people is informed by health care services, whose main task is to prevent physical deterioration. This aims to avoid patients becoming practically reliant on informal caregivers or formal services to carry out everyday tasks of life.

A range of recent research suggests that we should move this medically oriented preventive stance to a stance of positive maintenance and promotion both of personal independence and also of interdependence between people in a local community (Audit Commission, 2004). An important UK research review suggests that when older people are asked what keeps them independent, they do not refer to physical dependence. Instead, there are seven main themes in their answers:

- Housing and the home, including having a safe, comfortable home, keeping the house and garden in good order, and the role of aids, adaptations, and assistive technology
- Neighborhood, being close to friends, shops, and other amenities in safe, well-designed towns and streets
- Social activities, social networks, and keeping busy, including social clubs and community groups, opportunities for learning, leisure, and fun
- Getting out and about, whether by car, bus, or other forms of transport, such as shared taxis or mobility scooters
- Income, including the availability of benefits advice and take-up campaigns to pay for new expenses, such as housing maintenance
- Information, from an independent source to help older people to navigate their way around the system and find out about the opportunities and services that are available
- Health and healthy living, including access to NHS services and to advice on how to stay healthy and increase fitness

So our starting point should be that we can prevent dependence by emphasizing older people's full participation as citizens in all the different aspects of their society. Social and health care services are only required to offer help when older people are not able to carry out the everyday tasks of living and cannot maintain social contacts so that they become socially isolated. Marin and Zaidi (2007) suggest that there are three different situations in which older people become dependent on others in this context:

- When they are living alone in normal houses or apartments and need a range of different services because of reduced ability to live a normal life after a period of illness and disability
- When they have mental or physical disabilities and are discharged from hospital with long-term care needs
- When they have chronic degenerative diseases that will progress to the point at which they may lose their autonomy

Health and social care, therefore, deal only with a very limited aspect of aging. Even so, other members of the older person's family usually help to deal with situations like this, so that the older person becomes dependent, first on a fit spouse, then on other family members who are available. Informal help may come from neighbors and friends.

There may be greater need for health and social care services because social change may mean that an older person does not live close to family members. Sometimes other local people are unable to help, or the older person does not want to convert a friendship or social contact into a support. As they grow older, people may also lose contact with potential supporters, either because they have outlived their friends or their infirmities cut them off from social relationships.

Financing Older Age Groups

The other type of dependence, economic dependence, arises because most living arrangements assume that employed people within a family support others who are not working. We looked above at different ways in which older people might finance their lives. Older people who have not provided fully for their retirement from work become dependent on other people. In less developed countries, they may be supported by other members of their family rather than formal pension or social security arrangements or social services.

Case Example: Family Support in a Developing Country

I visited a developing country in South America and met Manuel, whose family owned a small farm. The farm had been operated by his father and mother as a joint occupation. When his parents become too old to carry on, it had been agreed that Manuel and his family would take over the farm without paying for the land, and in return Manuel and his brothers built a cottage for his parents to live in. Manuel provided food from the farm to his parents. The parents continued to do small jobs on the farm as long as they could. Manuel could not imagine accepting a system whereby his parents would have to receive long-term care through social services or a care home; care of his parents was his moral, religious, and social responsibility.

Such informal arrangements are used in most societies to sustain older people who are unable to provide fully for their needs. They are based on a system of family and community exchange and reciprocity: family and community citizenship. There is a fear that in many developed countries there is no practical way of continuing this as older people may be cut off from family and other contacts by labor mobility and lack of contact with the means of living.

Case Example: Retirement in a Transition State

I visited a country in Eastern Europe during the 1990s, when it was experiencing a transition from a communist to a market economy. In one town I met Elka and her husband, who were receiving a retirement pension after a lifetime of work in local factories and offices. Economic change had led to inflation, which meant that the pension was inadequate for their needs. They managed this through a network of contacts with family and friends who had small farms where they could keep animals and grow food. Elka and her husband traveled out to their friends' homes every day to help with the farms and, in return, received supplements of food that would otherwise have been unaffordable. An older friend of Elka's who was on her own also lived on an inadequate pension but was too ill to help in this way and had no family members left who could help her. For a while, she had subsisted by selling her jewelry and property but soon had been forced to ask friends and neighbors for help, and eventually to beg on the street. Elka tried to help her with some food.

Pensions are paid for either by financial transfers from the present working population through a pay-as-you-go scheme paid for by taxation or through financial transfers from people's working life, through savings and pensions. However, if financial changes mean that the value of pensions or savings decrease, or pay-as-you-go transfers become less affordable because there are not enough people in the working population to pay for increasing numbers of older people, it may be impossible to sustain a reasonable quality of life for older people.

Case Example: Barry Lost His Pension

Barry built up a good pension in his employer's scheme over a 40-year working lifetime. He and his wife looked forward to a happy and secure retirement. Shortly before his retirement, however, his employer's company went bankrupt, and Barry found that much of the pension he had saved for had been invested in the company's shares. The value of his pension was substantially reduced, and they were unable to afford their family home, which they had to sell to finance further investments to provide an income for the future.

The present economic system for the dependence of a rising population of older people leads to personal uncertainty for individuals and wider social insecurity. Long-term projections suggest that population across the EU will be about the same in 2060 as in 2010. However, during this period the EU will move from having four working-age people (aged fifteen to sixty-four) for every person aged over sixty-five to a ratio of only two to one. Most of this change will happen between 2015 and 2035, because people born during the post–World War II baby boom will be becoming more frail. The working population will increase until about 2020. This has led EU states to develop social security and social care service reforms, in particular, extending the normal period of working life by raising the age at which people retire from work. Raising the age at which retirement pensions become payable is important, but not the only factor, in this change. This is because many people retire or start to work part-time before the state retirement age or, on the other hand, may go on working after the pension would be payable. There will be an increase in the proportion of the population that is working (the labor market participation rate), and immigration will also increase employment in some countries, but generally the working population will fall, and productivity in all sectors of employment will have to increase if there is to be economic growth.

As the working population decreases and the retired population increases, there will be a decrease in tax income from working people at the same time as an increase in public expenditure as the need for social security and welfare for older people increases. High public expenditure increases are expected in Luxembourg, Greece, Slovenia, Cyprus, Malta, the Netherlands, Romania, Spain, and Ireland, although in some cases this is from a low level. Medium public expenditure increases are expected in Belgium, Finland, Czech Republic, Lithuania, Slovakia, the United Kingdom, Germany, and Hungary. Fairly low increases are expected in Bulgaria, Sweden, Portugal, Austria, France, Denmark, Italy, Latvia, Estonia, and Poland. Most EU states have tightened eligibility for pensions and social security benefits. Bulgaria, Estonia, Latvia, Poland, and Sweden have implemented major pension reforms, including a partial switch from public to private pension schemes. Less generous pensions are likely to lead to more aging people remaining in employment, although this may not be possible for older people experiencing ill health, and economic conditions may not make work available for them.

Health care and long-term social care expenditures are also expected to rise, even though, as we have seen, it only provides for a very limited part of need in older age groups, and healthier living may reduce costs. However, we have seen that most care for older people is provided informally in families and communities. Therefore, changes in family structure, such as reductions in the size of families, increased levels of divorce, and higher employment rates, will affect how care can be provided and may increase demands on public expenditure. Putting increasing pressure on younger working people to finance and support older people may lead to intergenerational conflict. Younger people may resist public expenditure on older people and resent the costs and pressures of supporting older people in their family. They may be excluded from having children and developing their own family life and be unable to afford housing because of the private or public costs of older people. Contrary to current media obsessions with younger people's interests, older people might become powerful as electors or consumers of entertainment. In this case, their interests may exclude younger people's interests and also cause resentment.

Most countries in the world also face considerable difficulties from the financial and economic crisis of 2007–2008. Increasing public expenditure to provide for aging societies may therefore be less easy than previous policy assumed, but private transfers through savings and pensions have also become uncertain. EU social policy has five main strategies to deal with this interaction between social and economic pressure, and these have an impact on policy for and practice with older people. They are as follows:

- Promoting demographic renewal by making it easier for families to have and care for children. This will help because if people are prepared to have more children, there will eventually be a larger population to support older people. Policies to improve work-life balance for families with children and to enable women to work, for example, by providing better child care services, are relevant.
- Promoting employment so that there are more jobs and people are supported in working longer. This will help because people will not be forced to retire early against their will. They will maintain a working income for longer, have more time to pay for a pension, and make fewer economic demands on the pension system. Again, this will lead to a larger working population to support the people who do retire.
- Making Europe more productive and dynamic, so that its economies grow and support social expenditure better.
- Receiving and integrating migrants to rebalance the working population.
- Securing sustainable public finances, which makes social security provision and equity between the generations easier to provide for. This means making sure that the tax system works well and expenditure is managed so that the increased costs of an older population can be paid for.

This range of policies makes very clear links between general social policy on the family, the economy, and social life and the position of older people and services for them. We cannot neglect the more general impact of the interaction between older and younger people in an aging society. However, the evidence suggests that we should also not exaggerate the trends into a crisis, since a wide range of social actors can make changes in their lives and so form a new social settlement.

Practice and Policy Implications

Social care services, even if most older people do not use them, will have to be organized to respond to the needs of older people in a period of cultural and social change in older people's role and position in society. There may be less political and social acceptance of the financial and caring responsibility for older people. There is a tension in how older people would like services to respond to them. They have usually wanted to maintain their autonomy of decision-making and independence in living arrangements from their families and from official interference. However, many have also taken for granted financial support and the availability of caring services from the existing retirement and pensions system, whether it is privately financed through insurance, provided through government services, or through family and informal care.

Social care services and social work practice need to be organized on the assumption that most older people will want active engagement and participation as citizens in their society in a good quality of life. This accords with citizenship social work values. Clients cannot be assumed to be dependent and disengaged, rather the opposite. However, there may well be considerable pressures on public services for older people and a greater use of private sector or self-funded alternatives. Even where private provision is an important part of the mix, present savings and pension arrangements may not be enough to provide for the amount of care needed. This means that there may well be disappointment and conflict at the center of the relationship between social work service providers, their clients, and the families and communities that provide informal care for clients. Inadequate services, whether they are public or private, negate the citizenship of older people.

Retirement

Why should there be such a concern with retirement age when I have suggested that this need not be such an important single point in people's lives? The crucial reason is that it marks an important administrative and social change. In particular, it may require an older person to stop paid employment, or others may assume that they should stop work. Connected to that, at retirement people lose the income that they receive from work, and it may be replaced by a lesser income from continued working and through transfer payments such as pensions or other social security benefits. They will also lose the respect that comes with making a contribution to their country's economy and to family income and resources, and feel the disrespect from others because they are economically and practically dependent. As a result, they may feel (and this feeling may accurately reflect social attitudes that we explored at the beginning of this chapter) that family members and others value them less highly than when they were working. This loss in social esteem may spread to other aspects of their life as well as making older people lose personal self-esteem because of their apparent dependence.

Retirement can be viewed in other, less stigmatizing ways. For example, it can be seen as like a "gap year" between school and university or sabbatical between jobs. It could be a period in which people can make an active contribution to other aspects of their lives. Examples are grandparents, uncles, or aunts caring for the family's children or disabled family members, enabling family members in midlife to maintain work and income. Retirement might be seen as a well-earned rest after a period of demanding work or as an opportunity to make a creative contribution as a volunteer, as an experienced committee member to local organizations, or as a community artist. We have seen that critical theory points to the emphasis in some societies on economic views that devalue retired older people rather than these more positive perceptions of older people's social roles and potential.

PHYSICAL CHANGES EXPERIENCED BY PEOPLE IN OLDER AGE GROUPS

The main focus of this chapter has been personal experience of aging, within a social context, because social work practitioners will mainly focus on people's experience of social change on their lives. However, those social reactions stem from physical changes, and practitioners need a realistic understanding of likely changes. Again, it is important to test out assumptions against reality. This section therefore moves to consider biological and medical approaches to aging.

PAUSE AND REFLECT: Physical Changes of Aging

Think about older people you know or have known in the past. What physical characteristics set them apart as older people? If you have known them for a period, what change took place that showed they were aging? Discuss these perceptions with other people if you can. What are general perceptions of the physical changes of aging?

Some Suggestions
Most older people experience general physical changes and also changes that are specific to their life experience. For example, the two mothers in the case examples above were affected by long-term disability and experience of a major illness in middle life. Positive life experiences can also affect us.

Although I have emphasized the continuity and variability of experience between people in younger and older phases of their lives, most people experience fairly typical physical changes as they age:

- Their skin becomes less supple and develops wrinkles.
- Changes in their metabolism mean that they develop visible changes, such as liver spots and graying or whitening hair.
- Most people experience changes in sight and hearing, which may have to be corrected or assisted.
- Physical reaction times and agility decline.
- Thinking and reasoning may become less clear.

There are a number of biological factors that medicine considers relevant to the aging process because they affect health care. These have little to do with the outward signs of aging that I have listed here, but mainly concern changes in metabolism, the way in which the body processes nutrients and manages physical changes (Martin, 2000). As people age, they accumulate minor changes in their bodies and various illnesses that have a greater or lesser impact on their lives. These include:

- A greater susceptibility to infection
- A greater likelihood of injury through falls and physical trauma and slower recovery from injury
- A reduction in energy requirements, leading to lower intake of nutrients and liquids, which may lead to poor nutrition and hydration
- Various metabolic disorders, in particular, an increase in the prevalence of type 2 diabetes mellitus
- Gastrointestinal disorders
- Cardiovascular disorders, including the development of symptoms of higher blood pressure, chronic heart failure, and strokes
- Respiratory system disorders, with a greater likelihood of chronic pulmonary disease and a bigger impact for any symptoms of asthma
- Disorders of the joints through the increasing impact of arthritis and back pain
- Genito-urinary system and kidney diseases, including greater likelihood of infection and sometimes incontinence of urine and feces
- Some mental disorders, depression, sleep disorders, and declining memory, cognition, or reasoning (Evans et al., 2000)

Should we worry about these changes? The answer is yes because, first, many of these physical effects are difficult to manage and add to the practical issues that older people and their caregivers have to respond to. Second, these problems lead to the four main medical problems of older age groups that are raised with primary care medical services across the world, which the World Health Organization (2010b) describes as the "four giants of geriatrics": memory loss, urinary incontinence, depression, and falls or immobility.

Also, cumulatively, they impact on communities. We can see an example of this in differences in survival in different countries. Michaud et al. (2009) examine changes in the survival of middle-aged people in Europe and the U.S. between 1975 and 2005. In 1975 Americans and Europeans would have expected to survive until around seventy-seven years, Americans slightly longer. By 2004 an American of fifty could expect to live to 81, while a citizen of a developed Western European state could expect to live to 82.5 years. Does this small difference matter? This is less of a difference than within-country differences that arise because of social inequalities, but if you cost a life-year at \$100,000, it involves a loss of \$150,000. The U.S. might save pension costs, but if this difference comes about because of ill health, the costs of health and social care and disability insurance or pensions might be higher. Illness has physical and emotional costs, as well. All the evidence suggests that the difference arises because of poorer experience of chronic disease and risky behavior in the U.S. "For example, Americans are about twice as likely to have hypertension, twice as likely to be obese, twice as likely to have diabetes, and nearly 50 percent more likely to have ever smoked" (Michaud et al., 2009, p. 4).

But why do these changes take place? Why do people age? Kirkwood (2000) points out that most animal populations also age, and therefore, aging can be regarded as a natural phenomenon, although it is perhaps affected by human civilization. There is considerable unresolved debate about genetic and evolutionary factors and also the possibility that the main factor is wear and tear, that is, where minor failures in metabolism or injuries accumulate to lead to larger problems.

Practice and Policy Implications

Responsibility for responding to the physical aspects of these problems falls to physicians and health-care professionals. However, all practitioners working with older people will hear from clients about physical changes and need enough medical information to be able to discuss clients' concerns with physicians and other colleagues. Many aches and pains of old age should not be borne in silence but may be treated or better managed with health-care interventions, or may be symptoms of more serious underlying conditions that should be treated. Effective hygiene and infection control is also important because many older people are susceptible to infection. This is relevant when working in older people's own homes and in care homes and hospitals where practitioners may visit. Physical frailty and ill health have an important personal and family impact that must constantly be balanced with social positives in citizenship practice.

Seeing aging in a medicalized way as decline may lead us into the trap of failing to recognize that many skills and capacities are maintained. Also, looking at the social positives of aging emphasizes the time and flexibility that retirement offers to do new things or things that we were unable to do or postponed when we were busy at work. We may benefit from greater self-confidence and experience of life, which allows us to manage our lives better (Hughes, 1995, p. 29).

Dementia and Mental Incapacity

Among the most important and distressing physical changes mentioned above is memory loss. The capacity to manage information in our brains varies over time. For most people most of the time, brainpower is enhanced by exercise. Keeping an active interest in learning and personal development will help everyone retain memory and mental capacity. However, there is often some decline as we age. Dementia is a range of physical and social changes that particularly, though not exclusively, affect older people. An authoritative statement in a joint practice guideline issued by the UK National Institute for Clinical Excellence and the Social Care Institute for Excellence (National Collaborating Centre for Mental Health, 2007) raises some of the problems of definition, as follows:

> [F]rom a clinical perspective, dementia can be described as a group of usually progressive neurodegenerative brain disorders characterised by intellectual deterioration and more or less gradual erosion of mental and later physical function, leading to disability and death. . . . Alternatively, from a social perspective, dementia can be viewed as one of the ways in which an individual's personal and social capacities may change for a variety of reasons, and changes in such capacities are only experienced as disabilities when environmental supports (which we all depend upon to varying degrees) are not adaptable to suit them. Moreover, dementia thought of from a clinical perspective (that is, disease and disability leading to death) may also prefigure our collective social and professional approach to people with dementia as people irretrievably ill and fundamentally different from able-bodied healthy young people.

Dementia affects about 5 percent of people over sixty-five years and about 20 percent of people over eighty years in Europe (National Collaborating Centre for Mental Health, 2007). We may take from this information that 95 percent of people in their sixties and 80 percent of people in their eighties are not significantly affected by it. Therefore, while it presents serious problems, it is by no means universal. Moreover, it is progressive, developing over time and sometimes being only one and not always the most serious of several conditions affecting an older person.

Marshall and Tibbs (2006, pp. 16–18) identify three main approaches to practice with people with dementia:

- Medical or organic approaches, the mainstream model, which focuses on and attributes all the problems that an older person experiences to the progression of the patient's underlying brain damage. The aim is to reduce the brain damage and manage the effects of it on the patient's life.

- Social approaches, which focus on the main impairments (failing memory, impaired learning, and impaired ability to reason) that arise in dementia that have an impact on the patient's social surroundings. The aim is to help the patient or people in their social surroundings to manage the effect of the impairments.

- Citizenship approaches, which emphasize the rights of people with dementia to participate in society and make a contribution to it, in particular using their creativity and other personal emotional strengths. The aim is to help people identify and maximize their strengths and contributions to their family and community.

Practice and Policy Implications

The approach taken in this book focuses on social and citizenship approaches, balancing them with awareness of and efficient response to medical issues, so that they may be managed to enhance the creative social opportunities in older people's lives. All of these factors are relevant to older people's health and social care needs. People are surviving longer because the development of technological civilizations means that human beings can manage the risks of life increasingly well and are living longer as a result. Consequently, they need to deal with some wear-and-tear issues. An example of a service to help with this is hip-joint replacements; most people who live a long time need help like this. However, they will also be affected by the tendency to age built into human beings by various evolutionary factors. Therefore, more longer-term care and help is needed for societies and the families and communities that make them up to manage the consequences of aging. This is the special contribution of social care services and social work practice.

MAPPING NEEDS IN LOCAL COMMUNITIES: AN IMPORTANT SOCIAL WORK RESPONSIBILITY

Since social care and social work practice focuses on contributing to family and community engagement with and informal support for autonomous older citizens, an important element of practice must be understanding community and family interaction with older people. Most practitioners work within local communities rather than at national or international levels. They therefore need to understand how these international trends are affecting their local community and to develop ways of understanding the changing needs of their local population in relation to aging and social care for older people.

There are a number of stages in mapping your local community:

1. Identify population statistics for the area and how these may differ from national statistics. What does this mean for the services required in your area compared with the nation and region?

2. Plot where people live on a map. What does this mean for the convenience, transport, and access to facilities and services? How will this change as they age?

3. Think about the housing types available in the area and their appropriateness for older people. Consider also whether there may be fuel poverty or general poverty issues that arise, for example, if homes are poorly insulated or expensive to run.

4. How does where older people live and their housing affect the contacts with family members and other potential assistance? How will access to health and social care, housing, and social security be affected by where they live and how they are supported?

5. What general social needs and specific needs for older people may be identified from where people live and issues about access to family, community, and other help?

6. What do we know about older people's wishes and what other people want for them? Possible sources of information are voting patterns and market research, either for health and social care organization or for commercial services.

7. What participation in decision-making and service-planning and design might be sought or possible?
8. What existing provision in each sector is available?
9. What potential changes might occur or be needed? Is new provision possible? How might old provision be adapted? What are the constraints and opportunities? For example, are there local organizations that might be interested in developing new services? Are there individual political or community leaders who might be engaged in working for older people?

CONCLUSION

This chapter argues for taking a citizenship approach to social work with older people. There are biological and physical aspects of aging that have important personal and social consequences, and practitioners must be able to make sure that their impact is well-managed. However, aging is a social process, as well, taking place within families and communities. Older people are equal citizens with younger people, and our practice must recognize the duty to sustain continuity and development in their lives and engagement with the existing and new social relationships that will come to older people.

FURTHER READING

Valuing Older People: A Humanist Approach to Ageing, edited by E. Edmondson and H.-J. von Kondratowitz (Bristol, UK: Policy Press, 2009).

An edited collection of papers exploring various aspects of humanism in relation to older people: an emphasis on spirituality and techniques such as life review gives it a thoughtful practical aspect.

Humanistic Social Work: Core Principles in Practice, by Malcolm Payne (Chicago: Lyceum Books, 2011).

This book sets out in a more general way the main theoretical underpinning of the humanistic citizenship approach to working with older people.

Pensions at a Glance 2009: Retirement-Income Systems in OECD Countries, by OECD (Paris: OECD, 2009). Retrieved July 5, 2010, from http://www.oecd .org/document/13/0,3746,en_2649_34757_47305613_1_1_1_1,00.html.

The Organization for Economic Co-operation and Development (OECD) is a think tank covering the economically developed countries. This is a useful publication on retirement and pensions, renewed every two years: summaries in various languages are available on the Web site.

Internet Information—Official

The main United Nations Web site on older people is the UK Programme on Ageing: http://www.un.org/esa/socdev/ageing/iyop_proclamation.html. The UN also provides links to national statistics Web sites, http://unstats.un.org/unsd/methods/inter-natlinks/sd_natstat.asp, and also to a variety of international statistical databases: http://unstats.un.org/unsd/methods/inter-nat links/sd_intstat.htm.

The European Union is mainly about economic markets. Therefore, the amount of social data available is less extensive than economic data, and what social data there are have an economic bias. For example, information on health concentrates on industrial accidents and health and safety. However, you can find population and overall health-care data. The Europa Web site provides access to information about the countries of Europe that are part of the European Union: http://europa.eu/index_en.htm.

Similarly, Eurostat provides access to population and demographic information across Europe: http://epp.eurostat.ec.europa.eu/portal/page/portal/eurostat/home. The country profiles provide information about particular countries. The Eures Web site (which facilitates job mobility in the EU) provides information about social security entitlements in each country: http://ec.europa.eu/eures/home.jsp?. Click on the "Living & Working" link and select a country.

Each country provides information about its social provision on the Internet, and this is often available in English. For example, the Polish social insurance office, http://www.zus.pl, has an English Web site, http://www.zus.pl/default .asp?p=1&id=1442, containing a summary of the Polish system of social care and social security.

Information about aging in the U.S. may be found on the Web site of the U.S. Census Bureau: http://www.census.gov. The current population profile, http://www.census.gov/population/www/pop-profile/profile.html, contains a section on older adults, http://www.census.gov/population/www/pop-profile/files/dynamic/OLDER.pdf, and an article on the elderly population, http://www.census.gov/population/www/pop-profile/elderpop.html. An article on current population projections provides information about likely developments: http://www.census.gov/population/www/projections/analytical-document09 .pdf.

The World Health Organization (WHO) Web site on Aging has links to many health-care resources in a variety of languages: http://www.who.int/topics/aging/en.

The OECD has a useful Web site for its aging and employment policies project, which gives access to useful information about population statistics: http://www.oecd.org/document/42/0,3343,en_2649_34747_36104426_1_1_ 1_1,00.html.

Internet Information—Unofficial

The American Association for Retired People (AARP) has an extensive site with useful advice on a wide range of issues for older people: http://www.aarp.org/. It promotes an active and happy retirement. Age UK is the British equivalent: http://www.ageuk.org.uk. Another useful UK organization is Counsel and Care for Older People, which has good information about services: http:// www.counselandcare.org.uk.

Policy issues are dealt with more fully in the information sources in chapters 2 and 3.

Integrating Older People and Their Services

AIMS

The main aim of this chapter is to place social work practice in the context of the wider range of services and facilities in society that older people use. These include ordinary commercial and public services for the whole population, as well as provision for vulnerable people, including older people. Research and policy development aims to ensure that all social provision for citizens is planned and managed to involve older people positively in community life by organizing services so that they are suitable for older people's participation.

After working through this chapter, readers should be able to:

- Identify three philosophies of integration in services for older people: integrated care, holistic practice, and mainstreaming and age-proofing
- Evaluate the role of generalized, low-cost services in maintaining independence and dignity for older people
- Explore three approaches to integration practice within social work: community and family integration, partnership practice with services, and macro practice to promote age-proofing and mainstreaming

PHILOSOPHIES OF INTEGRATION IN SERVICES WORKING WITH OLDER PEOPLE

Integration of Services

One of the important ideas about services for older people in recent years has been the policy of integrated care, originating in the U.S. during the 1980s and spreading across the world. It proposes that we should not focus only on specialist areas, such as social or health care. Another aspect of this is to integrate the range of services for a particular group, such as older people, including at least health, social care, housing, transport, social security, education, leisure, and community facilities.

An obvious way to build integrated care is to merge services or aspects of them together. However, this may mean that we lose specialist expertise or organizations lose focus because they have too wide a remit. An alternative is to create integrated care pathways so that people with particular conditions have a clear route through a range of services.

Holistic Practice

Citizenship social work practice connects with the integration objective in social care because it is a holistic practice. Rather than starting from service organization to promote integration, it looks to professional practice. Holistic practice focuses on how older people live as citizens in their social environment, rather than on particular problems or issues that they face. Holistic practitioners work with them as complete human beings, including social relationships and networks. One implication of holism is to balance the many positives and opportunities in older people's lives, such as wisdom, experience, time, and opportunity, against negatives, such as increasing frailty. Citizenship social work is a holistic practice that stresses the responsibility of everyone in society and organizations, particularly of the state, to recognize and develop older people's human rights, shared with all other human beings, to ensure that they are not devalued by aging. Since social workers are also human, they are equal with the older people that they serve.

The European social model, in which states accept responsibility for extensive support of vulnerable population groups, takes integration ideas beyond connecting services or attitudes to practice. Care services are seen as part of a wider range of public, private, and third-sector services. A mainstreaming or age-proofing approach says that care should not be the main focus of policy and provision for older people. This is because older people are full citizens entitled to comprehensive access to every aspect of a fulfilling life. We should aim at their inclusion in the community, not specialist provision that excludes them or help for them because they are excluded. Also, organizationally, all public, private, and third-sector services cover a range of responsibilities and should include older people in the full range of provision, instead of shifting all their needs into a ghetto called "health and social care."

Aging in place (sometimes called aging in home, particularly in Canada) is an American concept, focused on helping people to remain in their own homes for as long as possible. For example, we can organize people's homes to cope with increasing frailty, finance adaptations to permit people to remain at home, and provide safety and other information. This idea usefully stresses the importance of place in people's lives. People, including older people, have often developed a long-standing connection with a place, such as an area where they have lived for a long time, their home or a favorite part of the home, such as the fireside or the garden. Practitioners need to respond to place preferences as well as more social connections such as family and community. A similar concept is ambient assisted living, a European Union project based on a Danish idea, which aims to help older people live in a preferred place and maintains their existing style and quality of life. An important focus of this project is developing new uses of information and communication technologies. The Web site http://www.aal-europe.eu lists links to these concepts.

An important European example is Carmen (Care and Management of Services for Older People in Europe Network), a project of the European Health Management Association (Banks, 2004). Its policy framework proposes that integrated care provision must come from a vision that older people should have a good quality of life and independence to control decisions affecting their lifestyle. Services therefore need to take a whole-system approach, which starts from the person and fits services to their decisions and preferences. The alternative, common but undesirable approach is to offer a menu of services from which older people can choose, without their having very much control over how, when, or by whom those services are offered. This may make services easier to manage, but it means that they do not meet their needs as fully as they might.

Case Example: Annette and Brian's Past Experience of Care Services

Annette and Brian received care services twenty years ago, when she first became seriously disabled by the effects of a serious degenerative neurological condition. They had canceled the service because the caregivers provided by the agency had not provided the right kind of help or built the right kind of relationship with Annette and Brian. As her disability increased, he became older and less able to care physically for her. They had been reluctant to ask for help again, but when this was forced on them by a worsening situation, the social worker had offered direct payments, so that they could buy and manage their own services. Although this would have given them greater control, they did not want to struggle with the responsibility of this, so they opted for the social worker to manage the care services.

In this example of integrated care, independence and control meant giving Annette and Brian the chance to refuse the highest level of self-management. However, it enabled them to make the decision and talk through the options instead of being faced with a standard service provision. This case is adapted from a research study by Cree and Davis (2007, p. 130).

AGE-PROOFING AND MAINSTREAMING

Chapter 1 identified the changing social settlement on aging and retirement as an important issue facing most societies. The World Health Organization (2010a) has developed an aging and life course agenda that tries to respond to these issues. It seeks in particular:

- Financial security for older people by having a universal tax-funded pension
- To provide access to primary health care aimed at preventing common health conditions, so that older people can easily use health-care facilities
- To develop age-friendly environments that encourage "active aging by optimizing opportunities for health, participation, and security in order to enhance quality of life as people age"
- To maintain social patterns, such as family links, that support older people

Such policies are becoming increasingly important across the world. Age-proofing aims to ensure that everyday services do not exclude older people. We can reduce the economic and social pressures of an aging society by organizing all commercial, public, and social provision to facilitate older people using them. This reduces the costs of aging because expensive special services are targeted at older people who really need them, while older people who can manage using everyday services are not put into a ghetto, excluding them from society. It also helps to reduce intergenerational conflict.

Case Example: Two Couples Need to Adapt Their Living Space

Greta and George lived in an old house that their three children had grown up in, but it had three stories, and as they grew older, they could not manage the stairs and were finding it difficult to use either of the two bathrooms on the second and third floor; they found themselves confined to the second floor. Their friends Anna and Peter also lived in their family home, but it was newly built following recent building regulations that required accessible bathroom facilities. They had a toilet by the front door, and as they became more frail, this was easy to convert to a wet room with extra tiling and a floor drain so that they could take sit-down showers there and still go out without having to negotiate staircases. Anna and Peter's home had been age-proofed according to a new policy, which meant that although it was a perfectly ordinary family home, it could easily be adapted if someone became frail or disabled.

Mainstreaming is also important, ensuring that provision for older people is more connected to the services that everyone can use. There may also be economic benefits to this, because services are cheaper to run if they can be used by the largest possible proportion of people. Specialization may be both excluding and economically inefficient.

Meldgaard (2011, p. 108) makes the point in relation to homeless people: "Specialist services are important in terms of support in crisis situations, but important as well is the possibility for entry into mainstream services because this helps inclusion and integration into the service of the wider society." This is also true for older people: using specialist services tends to exclude people from everyday services. It is therefore important that social workers try to get non-specialist services for the older people they work with first. If they are forced to use specialized services, they should take care to link them carefully with mainstream services.

The UN's position paper on mainstreaming aging in social development states, "Successful mainstreaming should lead to (a) greater social integration of a particular group and (b) to the inclusion of a particular issue into all aspects of social, political, economic, and cultural life" (Venne, n.d., p. 1). In this paper, the UN Programme on Ageing proposes that we should seek to develop societies for all ages that are multigenerational and holistic. Accepting such aims means working toward services that ask: Do we facilitate older people to be a full part of society? Do we bring younger and older people together?

Older people often have multiple needs in a range of different areas of their lives. Where people experience multiple needs, policies and services need to tackle the multiplicity, not just focus on one or two of specialist interest to a particular agency. This argument is the basis of person-centered care, rather than having care based on a menu of services that may not fit together in a way that works for the individual.

Because, as we saw in chapter 1, older people are not a category of people "with problems," they cannot be picked out from the general population as having special problems, such as a diagnosed illness or identifiable mental or physical disability; they are citizens who may sometimes need special help. They, and generally their families, communities, societies, and governments, would prefer to be able to call on the services that everyone needs and uses first. One of the difficulties of services for people "with problems" is the dependence issue we looked at in chapter 1: services become stigmatized because the people who use them "cannot manage on their own," and then all similar people are categorized in this way also.

In most countries, social care services are part of local government. The reason for this is that they are part of provisions that citizens together, working through their local, regional, and national governments provide collectively for each other. Some of those services are universal: like policing, fire, and community safety, refuse collection, libraries, leisure facilities, and public health. Others are provided to people who need them at some stage in their lives: education, housing, social security, and social services are like this. Many of these services are provided informally: we all educate our children, lend and borrow books, take care of our property, save money for the difficult periods in our lives. All such services are also entwined in private provision—services that people buy because they want or need them and that are available from profit-making providers—we insure ourselves against death or disability, buy books, pay to go swimming or use the gym.

Because of the way social care services are part of much wider systems of social relationships, institutions, and the economy, we have to think carefully about how care services should connect with them and whether they encourage integration and solidarity between younger and older people or categorization and exclusion. Older people continue using mainstream services and social arrangements because, as we have seen in chapter 1, there is no clear boundary between their previous social position and becoming an older person. Moreover, older people's personal experience of their lives is continuous; there is no break between being middle-aged and being older. Social work with older people therefore takes place within the context of a range of services and provisions aimed at everyone in the population.

Case Example: A Local Planning Process

There was a consultation about local town planning in a region of the city. All local government services were approached, and the social care office arranged consultative meetings with older people. They commented about the rarity of public seats in the street to enable older people to stage their journeys to shops and bus stops. They also commented on the many bus stops that had no seating or shelter in rain. Most other organizations commented on zoning decisions and opposition to housing and shopping developments, and the older people had made suggestions that were practical and brought particular benefits for them.

This is an example of mainstreaming: it made sure that older people were engaged in an ordinary democratic process, but brought them together, so that their particular point of view could have influence. It also drew attention to particular needs that could be addressed in the context of wider services.

We saw in looking at the experience of age cohorts in chapter 1 that in many Western societies, older people have lived through and taken part in the development of a consumer society. Rees Jones et al. (2008) analyze this by suggesting that people retiring now have shifted from being passive to active consumers. What they mean by this is that most people are increasingly not willing just to accept what they are offered, but have become accustomed to a society in which they are entitled to make their own choices. We must question whether this is completely universal, for two reasons. One is that people whose lives have been spent in poverty or who come from oppressed minorities may have experienced substantially less freedom of choice than middle-class groups. Indeed, they may have become suspicious of offers of choice because their experience is of being excluded from choice by their poverty or discrimination against them. People in this position may prefer universal or mandated services because they are sure they are getting a fair share. The second reason is that different nations have had differing experience. For example, transition economies in Central and Eastern Europe may have experienced mandated services and less consumer choice in the communist era of administration, from the 1940s to the 1990s. Consequently, they may be unaccustomed to making choices and may have high expectations of fair distribution of services, even if these do not meet an ideal standard.

Case Example: An Older People's Information Service in Poland

I visited the central office of an older people's information service in a Polish city. It was run by a very small staff and some volunteers. There was a telephone information service provided mainly by one staff member, which relied on connections with local associations for older people in each locality in the city. While attempts to create active older people's groups had been tried, the generation of older people whose adulthood had been during communist times had become accustomed to having services provided for them. They used the local associations as an information service and as a social provision rather than as a structure in which they could proactively improve mutual support to each other.

Moreover, in consumer societies, choice is individualized. We assume that everyone will have the freedom to pick from a wide range of provision. This may work in a large retail supermarket, where there are large numbers of shoppers who might make different choices. But services for older people may be fairly complex, and it is sometimes hard to understand the different combinations, so how can we facilitate the individualized choice that many people have come to expect?

The mainstreaming and age-proofing answers to this question are:

- Start by not providing care in a way that separates older people into a service ghetto called "care for older people."
- Then go on to include older people into the same choices that everyone else makes.

Case Example: What Do I Do Now?

I was approached by an older woman after speaking to a local community association. She had been a very active citizen and managed many of her own affairs but now had cancer and felt that she would soon die. Her doctors were not telling her about this, however, only talking about the various treatments they were trying. She was frightened that these would be unpleasant and did not know what would happen. I talked to her and her daughter and suggested they think about what was happening as a pathway. There were a series of treatments: they could map these out by talking them through with the doctor. They could think about things that she wanted to do while she was debilitated by the treatments and get some clues from the doctor about how much freedom she would have to be active afterward. They could think of several things that she wanted to do, including visits to relatives abroad. Finally, she could think about planning for services if the treatments were unsuccessful and also tasks she could pick up for that stage of her life.

Generalized Services Contribute to Independence and Dignity

A UK Audit Commission Report (2008) looked at the costs of initiatives with older people. It noted that three areas of integrative practice were free or low-cost and benefited all or most older people in the community:

- Understanding, engaging, and mobilizing the local community
- Age-proofing mainstream services
- Providing good information

These were not very costly because local government was doing many of these things anyway: the need was to do them with an awareness of older people and their needs. Social work practitioners can feed into local decision-making in a positive way to achieve this.

Another service was low- to medium-cost and still benefited a substantial group of the population:

- Services to promote independence

Local government also provided social care services, but these were high-cost and provided only for a small number. Moreover, community-oriented services helped to prevent older people needing social care or strengthened their informal caregivers in the family and community.

A crucial aspect of achieving this was to engage local people and let them set the lead for the kind of change that they most wanted. Collecting local information from a variety of sources was also helpful. This included mapping the community for demographic information, consulting older people about barriers to using services and the services they wanted but could not get, providing information specially adapted for older people, and targeting groups likely to be in most need (the approach suggested for social workers and their teams in chapter 1). These groups included people aged eighty or more years; living alone; with no access to a car and who never used public transport; living in rented accommodation; on a low income or who had benefits as their main income; and with no access to a telephone.

A helpful strategy was to identify a champion or champions from the local community who did not have official positions but were prepared to be active in thinking about and organizing to provide services and support for older people.

INTEGRATION PRACTICE IMPLICATIONS

These broad policy ideas can be integrated into social work practice in three main ways:

- Working with individual older people in a way that integrates them with their communities and families
- Working with partner services in an integrated way
- Developing practice that permits age-proofing and mainstreaming by other services

Integrative Practice

All people, including older people, have rights to maintain and develop a family and community life. Many therapeutic approaches to social work emphasize interaction with individuals about their own feelings and reactions. A useful addition to this is thinking through how they want to manage their relationships with others.

A useful starting point for integrative practice is, therefore, integrating present experience and future plans with past family and community experiences. This involves looking first at important relationships and then at important activities with a view to maintaining or reconnecting with them.

Case Example: Going to Church or Seeing the Grandchildren

Maisie was an active member of her local church; she attended every Sunday and took part in a club for older people there, having lunch at the club twice a week. Her social worker assessing her needs for services asked her, "What is the main thing on your mind at the moment?" The answer was that it was impossible to get to see her grandchildren, who lived in a nearby town, because their parents had very little money, worked difficult shift patterns, and could not afford the time to bring the children to see Maisie, who was now housebound. The social worker asked how Maisie got to church and the club. A rotating group of church volunteers took housebound members to services and the club. The social worker suggested that the organizer of the group might be able to find a volunteer to take Maisie to see her grandchildren perhaps once a month instead of church; she would not miss too much, and maintaining her family contact was just as important. The transport organizer later contacted the social worker to get advice about insurance coverage for extra journeys at a long distance, but eventually this arrangement turned out to be possible. Later still, the church set up a volunteer transport scheme for several of its older members who needed transport to get around. The social worker also advised them about grants for transport for disabled people, since many members had various frailties and disabilities.

Another aspect of integration is building interventions over time so that they connect with each other. This partly reflects the need to focus on clients' and informal caregivers' priorities first. Success in a few limited initial aims often leads to trust in the practitioner for more ambitious developments. Many clients start with practical or financial requests, and these demonstrate tangible results, which may lead to more complex areas. Moreover, older people have many connections within their social networks, and resolutions in one part of these may bring other helpful changes.

Case Example: Money and Then Relationships

Mrs. Jensen was an informal caregiver providing a great deal of support to her elderly mother. The social worker was able to offer some additional services to give her some respite from her mother's care. Eventually, Mrs. Jensen asked about her own social security allowances, having seen the social worker obtain more benefits for her mother. The social worker gave some advice and made some referrals, which improved Mrs. Jensen's income. Later, Mrs. Jensen came to see the social worker at her office, rather than talking to her at her mother's house, and revealed that her husband was being violent toward her and her child. The social worker was able to refer her to a social worker for a women's refuge. However, to her surprise, the outcome of this was that Mrs. Jensen was able to talk to her mother about her relationship problems for the first time, and she and her daughter moved into her mother's house; this led to both social workers helping the whole family in various ways.

A third integrative practice approach focuses on citizenship as a way of organizing our practice thinking. A useful starting point is entitlement: citizens are entitled to appropriate social care and social work because we are all responsible individually and as part of our shared citizenship for each other. The next point is respect and dignity: citizenship requires everyone, including professional care service providers, to respect other citizens' dignity as individually equal with each other.

Dignity is an aspect of a person's being; a property that he or she possesses as a human being. Nordenfelt (2009) suggests that dignity is a scale by which we measure how we value people; it measures the extent to which we think them worthy of respect. There are four aspects to this. One is whether we think they have merit, that is, whether they are people who have features in their personal identity that we value in some way. Another aspect is people's moral stature and, connected to this, a third aspect, the extent to which they have self-respect. These ideas refer to whether we and they think they behave well in general and in the particular circumstances in which we meet them. Such ideas also refer to whether people have integrity: does how they appear to us through what they do reflect what they say they believe? A further aspect of dignity is the extent to which people have and are able to maintain and communicate a sense of their continuing personal identity. It is clear that dignity varies: it can grow and decline and is connected both to how we are and how we present ourselves as well as to how others perceive us.

It follows that in social and health care, we can help people grow or decline in dignity, and how we perceive and treat them has an effect on their own feelings of dignity and self-respect. This is, in turn, intimately connected with their personal identity. If we can help them enhance and communicate personal identity, they will have and we will perceive and treat them as though they have greater dignity. Personal identity is also connected with personal control. The greater control people have over their lives, the stronger will be their moral stature, dignity, self-respect, and personal identity.

This is particularly important in social and health care for older people because people's bodies represent and demonstrate their identity gained through the accumulation of their life experience. How we care for their bodies demonstrates our respect for their identity and dignity (Bullington, 2009). Through relieving people's symptoms in health care or offering a personal relationship and caring about and responding to their practical needs in social care, we help them maintain their integrity and continuity as a person and therefore their dignity (Ternestedt, 2009).

Case Example: Physical Caregivers and a Welfare Rights Worker

Mrs. Reynolds was a very old, disabled woman receiving regular visits from caregivers to assist her to get up in the morning, go to bed, dress and undress, and bathe regularly in her home. There were several caregivers who took part in this on shifts. On two occasions, she was visited by a welfare rights worker to check that her pensions and social security benefits were correct. She said to her social worker that, although the personal caregivers were competent, they only chatted socially to her as they did their work, and looked away as they dressed and bathed her; she felt they treated her as a task, rather than as a person. However, the welfare rights worker had talked about her life and opinions, for example, about having to claim social security after a lifetime of work, and Mrs. Reynolds felt that, even on brief acquaintance, she had made a personal relationship with her. The social worker pointed out that many people providing intimate personal care purposely kept a little distance because this reduced embarrassment. Mrs. Reynolds felt embarrassment about her aging body and understood this. However, she felt more dignified when helped to present herself well by one caregiver, who looked at some old photos in the bedroom and talked about how she dressed fashionably when younger.

This is an example of maintaining dignity in practice, by connecting with the older person's individual identity and history, rather than treating her neutrally. A research review of European studies in various countries (SCIE, 2006) came up with five elements:

- Respect shown to people as human beings and as individuals, shown by courtesy, good communication, and taking time and trouble
- Privacy, so that people have personal space—paid and informal caregivers enable people to have modesty and privacy in personal care, and their treatment and personal information is kept confidential
- Self-esteem, identity, a sense of self and self-worth, promoted by all the elements of dignity, but also by all the little things—a clean and respectable appearance, pleasant environments—by choice, and being listened to
- Freedom from unnecessary pain, including chronic pain—recognition that pain is avoidable and treatable at all ages
- Autonomy, including freedom to act and freedom to decide, based on clear, comprehensive information and opportunities to participate

As a result, the review identifies eight main factors in caring practice that maintains people's dignity:

- Enabling people to make choices about the way they live and the care they receive
- Speaking to people respectfully and listening to what they have to say—ensuring clear dialogue between workers and services

- Providing a choice of nutritious, appetizing meals that meet the needs and choices of individuals, and support with eating where needed
- Ensuring that people living with pain have the right help and medication to reduce suffering and improve their quality of life
- Enabling people to maintain their usual standards of personal hygiene
- Enabling people to maintain their independence by providing "that little bit of help"
- Respecting people's personal space, privacy in personal care, and confidentiality of personal information
- Supporting people to keep in contact with family and friends and to participate in social activities (SCIE, 2006)

Case Example: Joanna's Pain

Joanna, aged eighty-six, was living in a care home because her dementia made it impossible to care for her at home. Her social worker, Kate, was visiting one day, talking to Joanna in the lounge, when Joanna shivered and Kate asked a care assistant if she would fetch a cardigan or jacket; Kate normally did not enter Joanna's room. The assistant did so, and as she was helping Joanna to put it on, Kate noticed that she was grimacing with pain; she asked about this, and the assistant said that this sometimes happened when Joanna was being dressed. Kate made inquiries, and as a result the manager of the home asked the doctor to investigate. This eventually led to better pain control for escalating arthritis. When Kate found this out, she also asked about physiotherapy.

This is an example of a social worker being an effective communicator: she noticed Joanna's communication of pain, and she was also proactive in respecting Joanna's expression of feelings. Practitioners can be responsive to clients' needs and entitlement to services, even though direct communication is not possible, due to disability.

Partnership Working

Partnership working in social work refers to three kinds of partnerships: between (1) practitioners, (2) clients, and (3) family members and informal caregivers. As we have seen in looking at integrative practice, social work thinking focuses on relationships with clients or, for example, in family therapy, with families where the aim is to change unhelpful family relationships. Working with older people raises partnership issues because family members may need more than help in their emotional and practical response to, for example, changes in relationship with a loved parent whose behavior is changing because of dementia. At the same time, they will be partners with agencies in planning the care for that older person and they may also be informal caregivers for that person.

Case Example: Katie Being a Wife as Well as a Caregiver

Kevin had become increasingly disabled, with his wife, Katie, providing much of the practical care for him. A charity arranged a holiday for them in a nursing home, since an ordinary hotel could no longer accommodate his needs. When they returned, Katie commented to her social worker that this had been the first time for many months that she had felt like a wife rather than a caregiver.

This is an example of the kinds of losses that caregivers often experience, although it is important to help them identify gains and pleasures, as well. But it is also an example where the family role of wife and the emotional aspects of Kevin and Katie's relationship had been changed by her adoption of the caregiving role. Social workers often help people by articulating and talking through these kinds of changes of role. Many people see caregiving as so much a part of their natural family relationships that they do not plan to deal with some of the consequences of becoming a caregiver.

Two important aspects of the integrative social work role with older people and their social networks are: exploring and identifying those networks together with clients and supporting caregivers. Various kinds of analysis may be made and included in records, including the use of ecomaps and network diagrams, discussed in chapter 4. Box 2.1 identifies some of the integrative actions that may be helpful to informal caregivers.

Box 2.1 Support for Informal Caregivers (adapted from Payne, 2009)

Helpful areas of work	*Useful interventions*
Build support networks	Help users and caregivers identify useful friends, neighbors, organizations, and past contacts, accepting that not all of these will convert to a caregiving role, but may be prepared to provide some help.
Relationships with health and social care agencies	Encourage caregivers to think about building (or repairing) good relationships with health and social care agencies in all sectors that will help them to deal with crises. They need to be seen as someone needing support and help, but not a complainer or worrier; they also need to rehearse and plan assertive consultations.
Financial check	Help caregivers check on social security and other official benefits and finances generally to ensure they are receiving their entitlements. If no agency can help do this, work through a reference book.

Box 2.1 *Continued*

Helpful areas of work	Useful interventions
Think about the home and get useful equipment	Help caregivers think through possible changes or jobs around the house and get equipment that will make things easier.
Combine caring with personal development	Help caregivers plan to take time to go on leisure- or caregiving-related courses, or to build qualifications for the future.
Get out and about	Encourage caregivers to take opportunities for education, social events, visits, and trips, both on their own and with the client, even if the topic is new to them—enjoyment and stimulation will result and freshen relationships.
Have fun alongside caring	Encourage caregivers to cultivate activities or talk that caregiver and client both enjoy.
Be prepared	Caregivers should be prepared for possible medical or other emergencies (have the contact numbers to call if the user has a fall or a sudden worsening), keep them informed about possible progression of the disability or illness, and be ready to cope with changes.

Partnerships between Different Kinds of Practitioners

This may involve working with other professionals (dealt with later in the discussion of multiprofessional working) or working with employees in social care with different levels of qualification or skill. For example, most people working directly with older people are practical caregivers, often women, with low status, poor rates of pay, and little training. It is important to listen carefully to care workers' knowledge of and practice with older people. Because they spend more time with them and are often engaged in more intimate caring than social workers, they will often pick up helpful personal information or observe changes in need or problems that practitioners are unaware of. As well as building the personal relationships that allow practitioners to do this, an attitude that concentrates on developing all staff members' personal development, thinking about and responding to the training needs can be helpful.

Case Example: Staff Meetings Change to Include Staff Development Benefiting Residents

A weekly meeting of care staff in a care home usually focused on management-led or organizational activities, planning shifts, and giving instruction. A new manager included two personal development items. One was the chance for each care worker in turn to talk about something she had done recently that she was proud of; some preparation in advance to help people select suitable material was necessary, particularly at the outset. The second was to identify one item a week that would benefit residents, to check on an entitlement or a problem that many residents faced and report back on the client the next week. This training device built up knowledge among care workers about the range of issues that residents faced, but also achieved a developmental goal for both residents and workers each week. An example was to check on any sight problems. This uncovered several people who had not had a sight test recently and who needed new eyeglasses.

Partnerships between Different Kinds of Agencies

Agencies may be hard to integrate if they come from different sectors of the economy: public; private for-profit organizations; and voluntary, or nonprofit, organizations. Organizations may also be led by different professional orientations: biomedical, social, or educational, for example. One way of responding to differences between organizations is to create structural relationships either at the level of the whole organization or between sections of it, or in a particular locality. These may include:

- Shared support functions, such as information and training, which brings economies of scale and access to scarce skills.
- Shared contract processes, which support cooperation by financial incentives. Either two or more organizations can issue joint contracts to others to do particular pieces of work, or can contract to make payments to each other to carry out particular pieces of work.
- Shared working, where boundaries and strategies are aligned. This might be done through joint committees creating plans, by appointing an employee to carry out work in both organizations, or by outposting an employee from one organization into a role in another.
- Merger, where the joint working achieves greater permanence and a single identity for users and workers (developed from Whittington, 2003).

An important form of shared working in health and social care are integrated care pathways. In this model of interagency practice, a typical journey of a client through the care system is identified, and the role of agencies at each point specified. We can see clients as progressing through a series of gateways, with a particular professional or agency responsible for assessing and deciding on access to the next element of the service. An example of an integrated care pathway is shown in the diagram in box 2.2.

Box 2.2 Diagram of an Integrated Care Pathway

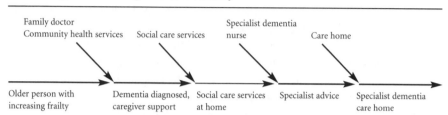

For practitioners, four partnership roles in working with other agencies are important:

- Liaison—making and sustaining contact with other agencies and colleagues
- Coordination—ensuring through liaison that the organizations work together when required
- Representation—acting on behalf of your agency or user with another agency or person
- Presentation—promoting and demonstrating the value of your work and the needs of your clients and other users of your service (Payne, 1993)

Practitioners should plan their work in each of these roles in relation to the partnerships they are involved with. Planning needs to consider:

- The nature, extent, and intensity of relationships required. Examples are frequencies of regular contacts, ways of making approaches to resolve problems, and how conflictual and consensual relationships are.
- Making the first approach, building an appropriate relationship around useful topics, and deciding on the time, effort, and other resources to be used.
- Establishing a pattern of relationships, how you will make contact (for example, through regular meetings or by telephone on particular cases), and the extent to which contacts will intrude upon the freedom of users and agencies to decide on their own priorities or promote involvement in other agencies' objectives.

The most obvious skill involved in all these activities is communication. The boundaries between organizations and disciplines are barriers to communication. Among the differences that may need to be overcome are different time frames, priorities, language, and jargon. Teams of practitioners can develop a program of partnership work with agencies that they work with regularly.

PAUSE AND REFLECT: Planning Relationships

Think about an organization that you or your team regularly work with. Identify the personnel in that organization and the different levels they occupy in the organizational structure that you have contact with. For each level, identify an appropriate contact within your agency, then review the aims of contacts, and, looking at the analyses of partnership roles and planning above, set out a structure of regular relationships and a plan of how you will develop them appropriately.

Some Suggestions

You will have to deal with situations where the objectives of each organization in engagement are different and where conflicts get in the way of well-structured plans.

Case Example: Applying for Grants

Nurses in one agency prepared applications for grants for care in people's homes for their clients. Social workers looked at the policy of the grant-making body and identified criteria that nurses could work toward in making their applications and helping the nurses to strengthen their arguments. Money got tighter, and nurses sometimes disagreed with decisions by the grant-maker that led to angry disputes, and the grant-maker complained to the nurse manager that cooperation rather than aggressive pressing of applications was the appropriate relationship.

Reviewing this situation, it was clear that nurses and social workers were aiming for the best possible deal for their clients, while the grant-maker had to manage a limited budget; their objectives were different. There was also a professional difference: nurses saw themselves as working for help for their patients through a shared process of professional decision-making with nursing colleagues in the grant-maker, while social workers argued that their role was to secure the best entitlement for clients through advocacy. The agency dealt with this by encouraging the process of shared professional decision-making between nurses in both organizations, while organizing to collect and take up disputed decisions through a periodic managers' meeting with the grant-maker.

Multiprofessional Working

Lymbery (2005) identifies three major issues in collaborative working between different professions, whether this is between organizations with different professional leadership or between different professions in the same organization:

- Professional identity and territory, in which the disciplinary knowledge or professional objectives differ. For example, health-care professions focus on biomedical knowledge and work with the individual patient, while social workers focus on social science knowledge and work with the family and social systems around their individual client.
- Relative power and status of professions. For example, doctors are often higher-paid, have longer professional education, and a stronger research knowledge base than social workers. Social divisions may feed into such distinctions: for example, the nursing profession is often mainly female, and doctors are mainly male, raising gender stereotypes of role and behavior. There may also be socioeconomic class factors: more doctors may come from higher socioeconomic classes than nurses.
- Different patterns of discretion and accountability. For example, the medical profession has developed a system of individual professional accountability for their work, and there are important legal duties associated with the decisions that they make, such as on pronouncing death or prescribing drugs. Other professions around them may be more obviously accountable to organizational and political policies and have fewer areas of individual professional discretion.

In addition, attitudes to professionalization may vary. For example, health-care professionals may see their expertise and caring role as important markers of the social value of their roles, while social workers may emphasize equality with their clients and demystification of expertise as an important social objective in their work.

Most organizations with complex groups of staff make arrangements to group people in teams and promote their collaboration. They do this through:

- Regular planning and decision-making forums based on teams that often work together, such as ward or community team meetings
- Reviews of particular aspects of practice, such as debriefing or "after event reviews" when there have been accidents, violence toward practitioners, suicide, or self-harm
- Educational structures to promote teamwork, such as journal clubs
- Formal team-building activities

Many organizations reserve more formal team-building for occasions where there have been relationship difficulties between members of a team, a change in organizational structure, a new development in work practice, or a substantial change in team membership (Payne, 2006). The two main ways of dealing with such issues in organizations are:

- Relationship-building work
- Knowledge-based practice (Payne, 2006)

Relationship-building tries to deal with conflicts, poor communication, and difficulties in making agreed decisions by getting team members to participate in agreeing to procedures and communication processes for transferring work and making decisions between team members. A recent German study (Jünger et al., 2007) found that good communication was the most important factor in achieving successful multiprofessional work, and role ambiguity and conflict were important factors in obstructing it. By working on these issues, teams develop an easy form of relationships in everyday teamwork.

An important aspect of this is mutual support. West (2004, p. 155) identifies three forms of support that team members can work on:

- Social support
  —Emotional support—including noticing and offering help when someone is distressed and upset
  —Informational support—being prepared to offer information to help a colleague, rather than keeping it to enhance your power
  —Instrumental support—practical help, such as giving someone a lift on a journey
  —Appraisal support—taking time to help people think through issues in their work
- Developing a positive and friendly social climate
- Support for individual team members' growth and development through training and staff development processes

Knowledge-based teamwork starts from the proposition that each team is a practice community (Wenger, 1998) that shares learning as they practice together, each contributing their particular knowledge and skill to the overall task. The role of leadership in this form of team development aims to help different people convey their expertise, rather than cutting it off because it does not fit with others' understandings. The team should aim to help different professionals pursue the tasks required to achieve good practice within their profession and put the different tasks together in an overall plan that includes everyone

(Opie, 2003). Each client's plan therefore would consist of some overall objectives that all team members would contribute to and agree with and then would record specific plans that would meet the professional duties of particular team members so that others would understand what they are trying to achieve in their work. As well as recognizing minority forms of practice, this particularly inclusive form of teamwork practice is good for recognizing and dealing with strains that arise because of ethnic, social, and gender differences between team members.

Research (Borrill et al., 2001; Payne, 2000) shows that teamwork usually has several important aims:

- Clear team objectives (a team mission or statement of objectives)
- Participation (an informal and cooperative atmosphere)
- Commitment to quality (always seeking to improve practice)
- Support for innovation (always seeking to identify new ways of doing things)

Within organizations, different professions can be helped to work together through "everyday teamwork" (Payne, 2006):

- Informal and social relationships, such as taking breaks with core team members, taking part in shared outings, parties, and other social events (peripheral team members have to work harder at these social connections than core team members)
- Informal interpersonal help with the stresses of work
- Participation in groups of people planning work with particular clients
- Participation in dealing with particular difficulties presented in the organization, for example, responding to help with difficult behavior from visitors

Age-Proofing and Mainstreaming in Practice

Social work practice with age-proofing means helping organizations that practitioners come into contact with to think through ways of adapting what they do so that older people may be included in their provision. Mainstreaming means ensuring that older people are, as far as possible, able to take part in ordinary life and decision-making. Sometimes people naturally do this as part of their normal response to caring situations. However, sometimes it is necessary for practitioners to alter organizational processes to make things happen. Leonie's case example, later in this chapter, is an example of this, and I take up the responsibility to change organizational expectations so that they respond more adequately to older people when considering macro practice in chapter 7.

PAUSE AND REFLECT: Review Mainstreaming Experiences

Review case examples in chapters 1 and 2 and identify examples of mainstreaming and examples where mainstreaming could have improved the services' response to people's needs.

Some Suggestions

Chapter 1: in my mother's case, a practitioner could have found acceptable social activities in the area that would have reduced her disengagement. In Uncle Brian's case, help with sorting out finances after his wife's death and in developing ways of living with his deteriorating eyesight would have improved his quality of life. His social worker probably accepted, in an ageist way, this deterioration as a consequence of aging, but it was because of an untreatable eye condition, glaucoma, and older people need to be offered ways of managing and maintaining a developing quality of life when problems like this arise.

Chapter 2: Annette and Brian would have been helped by finding non–social care services that supported them when they first refused services. Refusal is not a sign that agencies should withdraw help, but that a different kind of help, based on clients' preferences, is required. Greta and George could have been helped to think through the possibilities of adaptations to their home, alternative bathing services, or a live-in caregiver on the third floor of their home, which they could no longer use. The Polish older people's information service could have engaged older people in wider community services so that they did not see all services they needed as coming from a specialist older people's provision, but as available from a range of different ordinary sources, such as general community centers.

Case Example: Leonie's Reception

Leonie was a disabled older woman recovering from a serious operation in a hospital ward. Her family asked if they could take her out in a wheelchair, and staff arranged this. However, there was some anxiety when she had not returned after five hours. Eventually, she came back to the ward very tired at about 7:00 in the evening, and staff asked the social worker to speak to the family. Talking to family members, she found that the family had in fact taken her to a granddaughter's wedding, and the family produced photos of Leonie in her finery with a glass of champagne at the reception. The family had decided, probably rightly, that this might not be approved of by the hospital and so had carried out a subterfuge. It did not seem to do any long-term harm; and it was a compliment to the social worker that they would talk to her about this, but not ward staff. However, at the team meeting, the social worker reported back and suggested that the team should think about how they would respond to requests such as this in the future and find a way of indicating flexibility to patients. Eventually, the patient information on admission was amended to ask patients and families to talk to staff about any family occasions that patients would like to attend, so that safe arrangements could be made.

One useful way of empowering individual practice, in a mainstreaming agenda, is for practitioners to see themselves as cultural translators between older people, their families, and other parts of the community. Many people have not thought how the different life experiences of their older relatives gives them varying cultural expectations in life and, therefore, preferences. Alternatively, they view the likely preferences of their relatives through the lens of their own experience.

Case Example: Two Sisters

Daisy and Gaye were the daughters of a manual worker and his wife, an office clerk in the 1930s. Daisy married a factory worker, had three children, did office work, and cared for her family. Gaye had been fortunate in her generation to go to university; she became a teacher, married a manager in a large company, and continued in her teaching career, taking on part-time jobs well into her retirement. Both developed cancer in the final years of life. Daisy experienced several periods of treatment, of increasing severity, was very frightened of pain, and died in hospital while in the middle of a course of treatment. Gaye received one period of treatment, which she found uncomfortable, but when her cancer recurred, refused further treatment, dying at home cared for by her husband and daughter. Gaye's preferences were partly because her middle-class life experience gave her greater confidence in negotiating with doctors and asserting her preferences, and she understood the progression of the disease, using the Internet and other source of information. She had also seen her sister's fairly unpleasant experience.

These two older people formed their preferences from predispositions from childhood and from their class and personal experiences. If a practitioner were to improve Daisy's experience, she would start from careful discussion and interpretation of evidence and information. As part of this, the practitioner would need to listen to her fears and wishes for her life, so that she could provide information about the alternatives in ways that addressed specific fears and preferences. Gaye could interpret neutral information for herself. To give Daisy equal citizenship, information about how she would experience the various alternatives needs to respect her cultural expectations and class experience. Simply leaving her to find out what information she needs does not help her to use it; simply providing what the practitioner considers appropriate information does not allow her to connect it with her experience. Translation of the information from the professional culture of biomedical and social care to the culture and experience of people facing life decisions is necessary to age-proofing services.

CONCLUSION

Integration is a major objective in providing services for older people, because support is often needed for many different aspects of their lives. However, I have argued that as citizens, older people should not have all their needs transferred to a ghetto of health and social care specialist services for older people. There are also problems in merging services of different kinds because specialist elements of merged services lose their focus and expertise. Instead, practitioners need to develop and use skills in various kinds of integration. This includes a practice that starts with asking: what do we need to bring together here? But it also should use techniques such as care pathways and various kinds of partnership between services and professions to achieve integrated practice. Mainstreaming older people's experiences so that their help comes from everyday, non-specialized services, and age-proofing services so that they are able to respond to older people's needs are also important objectives. Social care is not isolated from the range of government and commercial services in every society; it needs to connect actively with and grow what is available in that society so that it is relevant for older people.

FURTHER READING

Social Integration in the Second Half of Life, edited by K. Pillemer, P. Moen, E. Wethington, and N. Glasgow (Baltimore: Johns Hopkins University Press 2000).

A useful collection of papers looking at different services and the need to incorporate older people in thinking and planning for them.

"Don't Stop Me Now": Preparing for an Aging Population, by Audit Commission (London: Audit Commission, 2008).

A useful study with practical examples of how UK local government has mainstreamed and age-proofed services for the benefit of older people.

Internet Information

The World Health Organization (WHO) Ageing and Lifecourse Web site, http://www.who.int/ageing/en, provides access to useful resources, in particular guides to health exercise programs and a toolkit for adapting primary health services to be age-friendly, http://www.who.int/ageing/publications/ Age-Friendly-PHC-Centre-toolkitDec08.pdf, many parts of which are relevant to social care organizations. For example, it discusses the principles of organizing age-friendly appointment systems, which help people who have memory loss.

Useful Web sites on aging in place include: the Ambient Assisted Living (AAL) Joint Programme of the European Union, http://www.aal-europe.eu, which develops information and communication technologies to maintain people in their own homes.

The Aging in Place Technology Watch is an American site that looks at innovations in a wide range of assistive technology: http://www.ageinplacetech.com.

Naturally occurring retirement communities (NORCs) are places that have developed into communities in which many older people live and have adapted to make better provision for them: NORC Blueprint is an interesting Web site for communities that want to develop better responsiveness to older people in their area: http://www.norcblueprint.org.

The UK Dignity in Care campaign, its research background, and a variety of resources for helping practitioners in maintaining dignity can be found on the SCIE Web site: http://www.scie.org.uk/publications/guides/guide15/index.asp.

Social Provision for Older People

3

AIMS

This chapter introduces the range of social provision for older people and discusses controversies about the role of social care in the range of public and private sector provision for older people. One of the important characteristics of social work with older people is its role in organizing and providing services, so practitioners need to gain a clear grasp of where social care fits into the services available.

After working through this chapter, readers should be able to:

■ Explore and analyze social provision for older people within a range of domains of service

■ Understand social care for older people as an aspect of social provision within each of those domains

■ Appreciate the role of health care, housing, and social security as crucial domains for quality of life among older people and, therefore, for social work intervention and participation

■ Understand the importance of welfare or assistive technology and telecare as part of care for older people

■ Examine the role of social work in integrating services for older people, including case management, cash for care, and services for informal caregivers

ANALYZING SOCIAL PROVISION FOR OLDER PEOPLE

Social and Economic Issues and Services for Older People

We have seen in the first two chapters that a range of policy issues affect how services for older people are organized in any society. Walker and Naegele (2009)

identify these policy challenges of aging societies in Britain and Germany. First, there is the need to respond to the consequences of demographic change for employment and the labor market; income, poverty and wealth; and in health and health care as they all affect older people. In nursing and social care, important issues are the extent of institutionalization; that is, whether older people should live in special accommodation and the lifestyle in such accommodation. Also, issues arise from some of the characteristics of old age, for example, increasing frailty and the approach of the end of life. Since the vast majority of people live independently in their own housing, the extent of their social networks and social support and their continued social and political participation is also important. This chapter seeks to place the role of social care provision within the context of that range of issues. In most countries, social care is the main location of social work practice, and social work in some form is often the leading profession in social care.

Social provision for older people may be examined in a number of ways. One approach is historical: it identifies how social care and social work with older people come to be differentiated from wider services. Koskinen (1994) usefully identified four main phases in the development of services for older people:

- From the nineteenth century to the mid–twentieth century, focus on relief of poverty, with older people included as a category of the poor, but increasingly becoming differentiated, so that specific provision was made for them
- Development of policy and services specifically responding to the general needs of older people as part of the population (for example, pensions, retirement)
- Development of welfare services and inclusion of older people as a category of people who received such services from the 1950s onward
- Increasing refinement of services and policy in response to social and demographic change from the 1990s onward

As part of these two later phases, social work practice and social care services developed.

Society's Social Provision as a Context for Social Care

Social care and social work always form a part of wider social provision, and we saw in chapter 2 that we should avoid seeing social and health care as the main site of provision for older people because most older people use ordinary commercial and government services together with family and community support to meet most of their needs. This is one way in which social work practice and knowledge spreads beyond their own services into wider social perceptions of what it means to care for older people appropriately. It works the other way: social constraints and expectations limit and motivate how social care services and social work provide for older people.

PAUSE AND REFLECT: Identifying Social Work and Social Care within Domains of Social Provision

A useful starting point for this analysis is a comprehensive formulation of the range of social provision with which social work services typically engage, made by Kamerman (2002). I have adapted her list of fields of social work practice to identify domains of social provision in box 3.1. In the second column, I give some examples of agencies that operate in that domain. In the third column, I give some examples of social work roles that might be employed within those agencies.

Box 3.1 Domains of Social Provision (adapted from Kamerman, 2002)

Domain	*Examples of provision*	*Social work roles within provision*	*Social work roles outside provision*
Health and mental health	Hospitals, community health services	Medical and psychiatric social workers	Community mental health centers, managed care for adults
Education	Preschool projects, schools, colleges, adult education, youth clubs	School social workers, youth workers, early years social workers	Child welfare, child protection, child care
Housing and homelessness	Public and social housing, housing advice, homelessness agencies	Housing welfare workers, housing advice workers	Housing advice, advocacy
Employment and unemployment	Job centers, unemployed workers projects	Advisers, community workers	Advocacy, activation
Justice, civil and criminal	Criminal and civil courts, citizens advice services, probation, prisons	Probation officers, adoption and children's guardians	Advocacy
Income transfers, social security, poverty	Life and care insurance, pensions, social security	Benefits advisers, welfare rights advisers	Advocacy

These examples are country-specific. Therefore, examine the agencies and social work roles within each domain and see where there are relevant agencies and roles in your country that should be added, and then whether there are agencies and roles listed here that are not relevant to your country.

Now look at the fourth column. Social work sometimes operates within social provision as a part of an agency whose primary role is, for example, health care, education, or social security. However, sometimes social work is provided in these domains by external agencies, or social care and social work agencies deal with issues that their clients have within those primary agencies. Column four gives some examples of these. Examining these, you may also be able to identify roles that in your country are inside the primary social provision or external social work roles that are not discussed here.

Each of these domains is relevant to older people, and practitioners will need to know about them in order to integrate services from each for older people. In your reflection, think about how older people might get involved in each of these domains and what kind of help you might therefore need to provide.

Some Suggestions

In some countries, services for older people are primarily within health care, and social workers would have a very limited role—older people in the community being helped by community nurses, for example. Also, in some countries social workers play an important role in providing discretionary social security—their involvement in managing social security decisions is an important source of referrals for family and mental health problems, for example.

In addition to social work roles specific to or not taken up by your country, some terminology may be unfamiliar. For example, "managed care" in the social work roles associated with health care is an American term referring to what in other countries is called care or case management. Since its main task is integrating services so that they are tailored to individual needs, I discuss this again later in this chapter.

Thinking about how the domains may affect working with older people, their health and mental health problems may change or increase as they age. Older people may think they have nothing to do with education, when continuing to achieve personal development through education may help them with problems such as social isolation. Countries such as Poland where social pedagogy is an important form of social work will naturally see this as a central part of the role. Housing needs and employment changes as we age and retire; how older people receive income changes; and anyone may be involved with civil and criminal justice; but older people may find it more difficult to defend their rights or to cope with legal demands.

SOCIAL CARE AIMS: QUALITY OF LIFE THROUGH APPROPRIATE PLACE, CARE, AND RESOURCES

A wide range of social provision is relevant to older people, therefore. Where does social care fit within that range? Most countries use the term "social work" to refer to both services and practice within them. Using the British term "social care" is helpful because seeing services as "caring" emphasizes the importance of interpersonal caring in services that enable people with long-term health conditions or social problems to live the best possible quality of life; and "social" recognizes that most care is provided by families, friends, and others in the community so that existing good interpersonal and social relationships improve caring provision and that supportive services increase the capacity of social networks in society to provide care.

Social care therefore focuses on three important factors within the range of social provision:

- Care: the support provided, its processes, and its objectives. How older people experience their care is crucial to a good quality of life: are the relationships and support appropriate and achieving the right outcomes? We saw in chapter 2 how dignity, an important objective in treating individuals as citizens, is connected with enhancing self-respect and personal identity.
- Place: the environment in which social care is provided. How older people experience the environment in which their care is provided is crucial to the quality of their lives: Is this the place they want to be? Does it offer an appropriate environment for providing good care?
- Resources: the relationships and economic help that facilitate a good place and good care. The resources of social care are human resources—good informal caregivers and paid care workers with the right skills and training—supported by the finance to provide suitable equipment and enough time for them to do a good job.

These factors are not just about lifestyle but quality of life, and crucial to understanding the role of social care is to understand that it is about maintaining the quality of life of the people it serves. The changes that take place as we age may mean that our lifestyle changes, because some things that were important to us when we were younger, such as parenting a young family, may belong to a phase of life that we have left behind, and bodily changes may make some physical activities less easy or impossible. Lack of age-proofing and mainstreaming may mean that we no longer have access to some activities that we would prefer to retain. Our preferences and interests may also change. For example, if we retire or change jobs as we age, we may lose interest in social activities connected with past work, or we may take up new hobbies.

In these ways, older people's lifestyles may change, although, as we saw in chapter 1, there will often be continuity alongside any disengagements that take place. Also, we saw that older people may reconstruct their social relationships and activities as they age. It is more useful to ask, even if the lifestyle changes: to what extent can older people manage to maintain their quality of life?

Quality of life is a slippery concept. It is not just about the economic standard of living, whether we are able to maintain the economic power to buy the things we want to buy as we age. This changes throughout life, and we manage these changes. The UN Development Programme (2009) assesses a human development index each year, which it uses to compare countries according to the extent to which they create a social environment in which citizens can develop their full potential and lead productive and creative lives that accord with their needs and interests. The annual reports examine more complex factors, for example, the report for 2009 looks at migration and the factors that lead people to move between countries and the social consequences.

The Human Development Index uses statistics on three elements of life to measure this (http://hdr.undp.org/en). One is a measure of average life expectancy, a proxy for the healthiness of a nation. Knowledge and education is measured by the literacy rate, the proportion of the population that can read and write, and by rates of enrollment in all forms of education. Finally, the standard of living measure equalizes purchasing power and measures the overall growth in the country's wealth. Countries are divided into those with very high human development: in 2009, this included Norway (1), Canada (4), the U.S. (13), and the UK (21). A Nordic country or Canada have, over the years, often topped the list. High human development countries include Poland (41), Mexico (53), and the Russian Federation (71). Medium human development ranges from Armenia (85) and Ukraine (86) to Nigeria (158). Low human development countries are mainly in Africa.

Quality of life comes up in many different services. For example, in 2001–2002 the UK Audit Commission carried out a project to help local governments identify quality of life indicators to promote the social, economic, and environmental well-being of their areas. They identified useful indicators, since updated, in three broad areas of economic, social, and environmental well-being, examples being factors in the level of social and educational deprivation (Audit Commission, 2005).

Using a different approach focused on older people, Walker (2005) compares the quality of life in five European countries, examining definitions of old age, environmental factors, and socioeconomic aspects of policy. Within these policy parameters, participation, social support, and subjective well-being are important aspects affecting how people experience the quality of their lifestyle as they age.

Taking these points together, quality of life is partly connected with people's economic standard of life, their access to education and personal development, and their health. We can add to that whether they have a good physical environment, are free from multiple social or economic deprivations, can participate actively in their society, have adequate social support, and have a subjective sense of well-being. This view of quality of life can apply to all of us as well as older people.

Since quality of life includes adequate support and a sense of well-being, it must also include appropriate social provision to secure this. Health-related quality of life measures are available for many physical conditions, and may be objective or clinical and holistic (Jacobs & Rapoport, 2003). Objective measures examine issues such as mortality, rates of cure, or survival. Holistic measures include people's perceptions as well as objective information. The perceptions may be an overall sense of well-being, how well people are in relation to an identified condition, or how well they are able to pursue some aspect of their life, such as ordinary living. McCormick et al. (2009) draw on examples from all over the world to suggest that maintaining and developing relationships, opportunities for work, and useful activity for learning and for living in an attractive and stimulating built environment are important for well-being in later life. Their examples also suggest that it is possible to devise and provide services that can contribute to well-being in this way.

Care, place, and resources—the crucial aspects of social care that achieve quality of life—connect with three major domains of social provision, which have important roles in social provision for all citizens.

THREE MAJOR GENERAL SERVICES: HEALTH, HOUSING, AND SOCIAL SECURITY

Older people often draw significantly on these general services available to and used by the whole population: health, housing, and social security. Social work with older people often involves making these three systems work for social work clients, and assisting these systems respond appropriately to older people's needs. Social care services are built into these major social provisions. Therefore, among the general domains of social provisions, these are particularly important for practitioners to understand and connect with.

Health

Health-care services become important to older people when disability, multiple illnesses, and increased frailty begin to affect them as they age. Box 3.2 sets out a basic model of health-care service relevant to many countries, gives a UK example, and then a description of the different aspects of provision.

Primary health care gives citizens access to health care and is therefore usually at local clinics or doctors' offices. Many European countries have polyclinics where a range of diagnostic and treatment services are made available at a local site. Secondary health care offers diagnosis and treatment for more complex conditions, particularly where a stay in hospital or an operation is needed. The boundary varies in different countries, as day operations, for example, may be carried out in a polyclinic, community hospital, or other community resource. Tertiary health care is sometimes available where specialized treatment and expertise is required. Intermediate treatment is a UK category identifying facilities for longer-term active rehabilitation to a community setting; the aim is to avoid people staying in long-term care when they could be enabled to return

Box 3.2 Typical Health Care Services (extracted from Payne, 2009, table 5.1)

Health care type	UK example	Description
Primary or community health care	General practitioner (GP) surgery provides a family medical service	First point of contact between citizen and the health-care system, providing assessment and most treatment
Secondary health care	General hospital, including psychiatric units	Accident and emergency services in large centers and base for assessment and treatment on referral from GPs
Intermediate health care	Hospital/community	Care to assess, rehabilitate, and return home patients who have had extended or complex treatment in secondary or tertiary care
Tertiary health care	Specialist hospital or health-care establishment	Advanced treatment for unusual or complex illnesses or conditions, including psychiatry and palliative care for people who are dying and their families
Continuing care	Community or home services or care homes	Care at home to meet a primary health-care need that would otherwise require hospital treatment

home. Continuing care is also a UK category, funding care meeting health-care needs in the patient's family home or a care home; the aim is, as with intermediate care, to reduce the need for hospital care.

Housing

Any person's quality of life derives partly from his or her living arrangements. During their lifetime, most people build a personal and family home, which moves with them into old age. One of the issues about old age is the changes in housing needed, especially as people require help with care. The ideal of many social care systems is to support care in the family home, in the community, rather than in special facilities. This is because most people prefer to retain their links with their family and local community, and this is also likely to enable them to best use family and local support if they need it.

Box 3.3 sets out the range of accommodation that may provide a living setting for older people. The starting point is people's own homes. Then the box

Box 3.3 Accommodation for Older People (adapted from Payne, 2009)

Accommodation type	Description	Service delivery
Your own home	The ordinary place of residence for an older person, usually the family home	Home or domiciliary social and health-care services, community, nursing, and mobile meals may be delivered in any of these settings. Older people may travel to day care and meals provision.
Sheltered housing	Housing specially designed for older people, which limits the demands of self-care	
Very sheltered or extra-care housing	Sheltered housing with support or care services easily available	
Adapted housing (for people with disabilities)	Housing with physical adaptations or facilities to enable people with disabilities to increase the level of self-caring that is possible	
Adult support services	Accommodation with an unrelated family	
Care homes, residential care, or old people's homes	Accommodation shared with others requiring care	Care is an integral part of accommodation, although retirement communities may offer flexible arrangements in the same accommodation.
Nursing homes	Accommodation shared with others requiring nursing care	

lists a number of assisted living arrangements; "assisted living" is a term covering a variety of living arrangements in which assistance is provided, usually in specially adapted accommodation, but short of the communal accommodation in care or nursing homes.

Social Security

A World Bank study (Holzmann & Hinz, 2005) suggests that social security systems should be multi-pillared, containing a number of different, interacting elements:

- Provision for poverty alleviation for all older people, meeting basic needs; this would be funded from general taxation. This would meet the needs of people who have a low lifetime income or little engagement with employment for reasons of disability or lack of jobs. It might also be used where disasters, natural or made by humans, lead to destitution.
- Provision for a retirement pension scheme. Prefunding, by transfer payments from people when they are in employment, is preferred because it provides better guarantees that countries will be able to afford the payments when they need to be made.
- A voluntary savings scheme for retirement. This allows people to add to their income in retirement through savings or by paying into an additional pension.
- Broader support to older people, including family support, access to health care, and housing.

How different countries implement these systems varies; a number of combinations of these are possible.

PAUSE AND REFLECT: Your Country's Pension Schemes

Using the World Bank pillars, identify the main points of your country's scheme.

Some Suggestions
I looked at my own position. The UK offers a basic state pension payable to all older people who have made the required number of contributions through work, or other contributions to society such as periods of child care (the first element of the second pillar); I will get this when I reach retirement age—sixty-five at the moment but set to rise. This is supplemented by discretionary payments,

a pension credit, if you meet the criteria, to support older people who do not meet a basic poverty level (the first pillar); I won't get this because I have other pension provision. There is a second state pension which you contribute to either through an insured scheme operated by your employer or by a fallback provision operated by the state (a second element of the second pillar); I have both of these. You can add to this either through tax-free savings or by having an additional pension (the third pillar); I also have some savings. There are heating fuel, housing, and council tax benefits, if you meet the criteria, to help with housing costs. You receive free health care and drugs from the national health service if you are over sixty, and a variety of other benefits are available to meet particular contingencies. These constitute the fourth pillar.

In most countries, there is debate about the appropriate level of payment and criteria for these benefits; among the issues might be meeting a moral requirement for a society to reduce poverty in old age, or to support particular groups of older people. For example, some countries provide additional support to former members of the armed forces. Some benefits aim to protect older people. For example, in some colder countries, payments to reduce or avoid fuel poverty may be important. Holzmann and Hinz (2005) suggest that useful criteria to evaluate pension systems might be:

- Adequacy—the system should alleviate basic poverty, aiming at smoothing changes in lifetime consumption. This suggests that whatever the wealth of your country, retirement or frailty should not lead to disastrous changes in older people's lifestyles.
- Affordability—the system is within the capacity of most individuals and the country as a whole to make their contributions.
- Sustainability—the system is financially sound enough to be maintained over a long period, making reasonable assumptions about national financial circumstances.
- Robustness—the system is able to withstand economic, demographic, and political change and natural disasters.

ANALYZING SOCIAL CARE

Social Care and Social Work

So far, we have examined the range of social provision and identified the focus of social care within that range as being about maintaining older people's quality of life through creating appropriate care in an appropriate place, using appropriate human and other resources. Within social care services, social work is the proactive use of interpersonal skills in engaging with people to support them, to help them achieve fulfilling lives, and to provide them with appropriate services. I take this approach in the next three chapters about skills, criticality, and creativity in social work practice with older people.

Case Example: Bereavement Care

A case example may help to explain these distinctions. Bereavement care is a service to provide counseling and interpersonal support for people who have been recently bereaved. Most people are able to experience bereavement and continue with their ordinary life. They make adjustments to deal with changed relationships with the person who has died; their bonds with that person will often continue but in a different form (see continuing bonds theory, discussed in chapter 8). Their relationships with other members of their family and community also change. For example, after the loss of someone important to an individual, other people may become more important than they were.

Some bereaved people are unable to deal with important emotions arising from their loss or experience difficult practical problems. For example, the sadness that is natural in bereavement may extend into depression or practical difficulties, such as loss of the deceased person's income, and may lead to anxiety. Help with these emotional and practical problems can allow people to recast their lives in a positive way. The experience of this will give them skills to deal with further bereavements and to respond more appropriately to other people in their family and community who experience bereavement.

Bereavement care services provide this service through one-to-one interpersonal help from helping professionals or volunteers supported by professionals, either in a counseling setting or people's own homes, through groupwork and by encouraging bereaved people to take part in organizations that might help them reestablish social networks.

Comparing this with the main aspects of social care services, bereavement care services provide a special place with a focus on the particular social situation of bereavement, including special places to develop counseling relationships and groupwork. They provide the support, care, human resources, expertise, and information to help people deal with this issue. The interpersonal work is done by helping professionals, which might include social workers. Social work in bereavement is about how to process and manage those interactions in such a way that they deliver the services needed.

Levels of Social Care Services

Most countries respond to these different aspects of care by organizing social provision at different administrative levels:

- Local level services to integrate with family and informal care
- In many countries, an intermediate regional level to plan strategy for the region and sometimes to provide services for groups of citizens who require specialized services
- National level services to create policy and to distribute resources

How this is worked out affects the culture and administrative arrangements of a country. For example, many countries are federal in organization: Germany has *länder*; Poland, *voivodships*; the UK, four main countries; and the U.S., states. These levels of administration often have considerable political autonomy and develop their own legislation and policy, particularly in matters of social and family policy. To understand provision for any social group, we need to analyze the relationships between these levels and the responsibilities given to different policy and service arenas. For example, many countries have a national system of social security, to ensure equality of payments across the country. In the U.S., there is both state and federal (that is, national) provision for various eventualities such as unemployment, while other social security provision is mainly or entirely federal; while in the UK and most other European countries, provision is universal, and national social security policy dominates. In many countries, there is an administrative distinction between discretionary social security benefits, where people have to be assessed for their entitlement and often means-tested, and insured social security benefits, where entitlement derives from having paid contributions. In the UK, this has little bearing on social work, since both elements are handled by the (national) Benefits Agency of the (national) Department of Work and Pensions. In many Nordic countries, this distinction affects social work more directly, since discretionary benefits are linked to local government social work services. Another example is health care. In the U.S., health insurance is largely private, although recent federal legislation aims to regulate this so that coverage is more complete in the future than at present. In the UK and most European countries, health care is substantially provided by the state, although there are various patterns of insurance. Different European countries also vary in the extent to which health care is provided as part of local government or through a national service.

PAUSE AND REFLECT: Your Country's Social Provision

Look at the system in your own country and compare it with another country, using information from the Internet or from a recent text (recent because systems change all the time). Try to draw a diagram of relationships and separate responsibilities. The benefit of comparing two systems is that issues arise that are outside your cultural expectations.

Some Suggestions

You can try doing this in two ways. One way is to draw a structural diagram, showing the national, regional, and local level provision. For example, the Polish social insurance institution (ZUS) identifies three different ministries responsible for labor and social policy, for agriculture and rural development (which makes provision for social security in rural areas), and for health (which manages the health insurance arrangements). The main categories of responsibility are set out as columns under the ministry providing for them. It then distinguishes various *voivodship* (regional) and *poviat* (municipal) responsibilities in each category of responsibility. This reflects a common feature of many countries with a substantial agricultural base, that special arrangements are made for rural areas. People from a non-agricultural country looking at social provision might not even think to ask questions about agricultural development.

Another approach is to set out the citizen's experience of applying for services. This is helpful because it identifies discontinuities that may occur in how services fit together for citizens. For example, in the UK, all citizens are registered for the provision of health care with a general practitioner, a locally based family doctor who meets most of their health-care needs, referring them onward to hospitals or specialist services for more complex needs. There is no registration for social care; applications for service are made to the local government authority covering the area in which you live. This is differently organized across England and the other countries, but in most cases concerns about older people are dealt with by an adult social care department. Some are part of larger housing and social care departments. So, unlike health care, the entry to social care is application for a service or referral by another professional to a local administrative center; there is no personal relationship as there is with the general practitioner.

ACCOMMODATION AND CARE FOR OLDER PEOPLE

Place and Care: Care Homes and Care in the Home

Since place and care are bound together as elements of social care, a useful way of understanding social care services is to see how care is connected with housing and accommodation. Since everyone needs to live somewhere, care services need to fit in with living arrangements; care and place go together.

Going back to box 3.3, the amount of self-care required decreases as we go down the list. Therefore, care interacts with accommodation, since types of housing are to some degree identified by the amount of care they include. In care and nursing homes, care services are provided as part of the accommodation. Otherwise, they are delivered to the home, or people attend day centers for meals, social activities, and health and social care services, such as information, advice, and interpersonal help. In adult support services, people are accommodated in other people's homes and might be supported there in their own self-care, receive some care from the people with whom they live, or receive domiciliary and day care services as required.

Care homes have a long and important history as an aspect of social care. As Western countries began to become industrialized and urbanized, informal and family community provision for people with difficulties in rural areas was lost. The response to this was to build large institutions for many different groups in society, such as poor or mentally ill people. During the twentieth century, these were the main provision for people in difficulties, particularly under the poor law system for dealing with poverty in many countries, which required poor people to live in workhouses to receive help. Since many people were poor because they could not work due to disability or aging, poor law buildings became like hospitals and care homes. When the poor laws were repealed in many countries, the buildings remained. There is thus a legacy of large, poor-quality, oppressive buildings with inflexible and uncaring regimes that do not provide a good place or good care. People were institutionalized, that is, their behavior adapted to the regime, and they lost independence of mind and action. During the last part of the twentieth century, many countries worked hard to provide improved environments and regimes. However, this is still patchy in many countries, not helped by the reality that there are insufficient resources to pay and train enough staff to provide a good quality of life.

PAUSE AND REFLECT: Your Care Services

Make a list of services available in your administrative area and classify it according to box 3.3. Identify whether there are accommodation or care arrangements that are missing in your area, or where you have additional types of accommodation and care. How would you evaluate each different type of accommodation and care service? Think in particular about the care offered, the place or environment that they provide for care, and the resources available.

Some Suggestions

Adult support services are fairly rare, so this might be a service that is missing. Evaluating current provision, you may feel that the care homes in your area do not provide well for particular problems, for example, dementia or some kinds of physical disability, that they have a rather static and unimaginative environment, or do not have enough staff to provide good interpersonal interaction with the residents.

Day Care

Day centers are part of the movement to displace the poor regimes of care homes because they allow people to live in their own home while receiving high levels of care in the day center. This may provide assessment, support, education, supervision and surveillance, opportunities for self-expression, rehabilitation and re-ablement, linking and integration with other services, and transition between more different stages of care (adapted from CCETSW, 1975).

Box 3.4 lists and explains different types of day provision that may be helpful in different situations. Among the difficulties in providing and organizing day care are:

- Transport—can older people get there and return home conveniently, cheaply, and safely?
- Location and type of buildings—are they convenient for staff and older people? Do they provide an attractive environment? Do they avoid institutionalization or inappropriate and stigmatizing contact with another service?
- Multipurpose centers—many of these different types of centers can be organized together, but functions may interfere with each other, or make them more or less attractive to attenders. For example, centers useful and attractive to people in their sixties may not be useful for people in their eighties.
- Integration with other services—is day care or treatment integrated with other community or inpatient services?
- Special or occasional needs—some people may need help for a brief time or when they are in transition from one service or situation to another; however, they can be hard to identify, and their special needs cannot always be provided for in more general settings (Morley, 1972).

Case Example: A Day Center in a Care Home for Older People

A day center attached to a care home for older people provided social facilities and support for frail older people. However, once people were referred there, no arrangements were made for their needs to be reviewed regularly, unless they needed to enter the care home. Some therefore continued when they became less frail, and a waiting list for attendance built up, with more disabled people being kept waiting. The center became more of a social center than a service to help people manage frailty. Also, the service was poorly integrated with services in

Box 3.4 Day Care Facilities (adapted and updated from Morley, 1972)

Day care type	*Description*
Day hospitals	Provide treatment and care that does not require an overnight stay. It is usually attached to a hospital or clinic with broader responsibilities. It may provide treatments that require nursing, medical, or specialist involvement and cannot be provided at home or may be better carried out in groups, with regular assessment and surveillance and rehabilitation or re-ablement.
Day centers	Provide social care, such as bathing or management of dressings, and social interaction and support.
Psycho-geriatric day care	Day hospitals or centers that specialize in people with dementia or disabilities arising from long-term mental ill-health.
Day care or social clubs in care homes	Day care provided as part of a care home. This may enable more economic use of the care home's facilities and also stimulate more interaction for care home residents and help to accustom day care attenders to the care home if they need to use it in the future.
Social centers or clubs	Social activities for a half day or less, often as part of wider social clubs or leisure facilities at community centers.
Shelters and rest centers	Provides premises in shopping centers and railway or bus stations that enable older people to have a period of rest and social contact, often with refreshments, as part of their daily activities. "Pop-in" or "drop-in" facilities may attract people who do not want the social life of clubs or centers and make it easier for people with disabilities or illness to continue ordinary activities.
Communal rooms in group-housing schemes	Provide premises for older people living in a group of houses for older people to have a social environment or alternative sitting area outside their own home. It may also provide a safe and pleasant environment for contact with visitors and friends.
Lunch clubs	Provide premises where older people can take a meal in social surroundings, improving nutrition, reducing social isolation, and reducing the demands of housework.
Work centers	Provide opportunities for craft or other activities, employment, or skills training.
Clubs and societies	Civic, church, or other social organizations that provide opportunities to meet, hear a speaker, and engage in joint social activities.

other ways. For example, nurses would travel to provide treatment in patients' homes, only to find that the patient was attending the day center that day. They could more efficiently have visited the day center to provide this treatment, if the systems had been in place to inform them of the attenders' days at the center. However, because it was not a day hospital, the manager tried to maintain it as a social environment and refused to allow medical and nursing staff to assess and treat attenders. The manager of the care home also discouraged attenders from entering the care home lounge, because he felt that too much integration meant that their full-time home was being invaded by more transient older people in the day center. These difficulties arose because of the multipurpose nature of the premises and the poor integration of services. They were resolved by a periodic review of the center's functioning as part of the wider service, by reviewing the objectives and style of the center, and finding locations within it where specialist treatment could be provided. New computer systems allowed practitioners from local health and social care services to identify attenders and their dates and times of attendance. As treatments became available at the center, there also had to be a discussion about how attenders' medical conditions could be kept confidential from other attenders.

Welfare or Assistive Technology

A recent development of services, which is likely to become more important in the future, is welfare or assistive technology (AT). A simple definition from the World Health Organization (2004, p. 10) is "any device or system that allows individuals to perform tasks they would otherwise be unable to do or increases the ease and safety with which tasks can be performed."

While everyone uses some devices that we can describe as AT, and practitioners sometimes call upon AT now, possible uses are likely to increase as research and development progresses. Box 3.5 groups different types of assistive technology according to Beech and Roberts's (2008) analysis, which divides AT into three main categories, refined by Milligan's (2009) analysis of types of equipment available.

Some of these devices, such as intruder alarms and remote control of electronic devices, are widespread and familiar. Alarms worn round the neck and connected to a control room are widely used and allow a measure of client independence because they only activate the alarms when they wish. Other systems permit the control room to hear what is going on in the alarm location or to speak to the person wearing the alarm.

Beech and Roberts (2008) identify the benefits that AT confers from research, which have to be balanced against potential concerns:

Box 3.5 Types of Assistive Technology (AT) (Beech & Roberts, 2008; Milligan, 2009)

Beech and Roberts's category	*Explanation*	*Types of equipment*	*Examples*
Supportive technologies	Help individuals do things that they find difficult	Environmental control systems	Wireless control of home equipment, hands-free phones, lighting and door warning systems
Responsive technologies	Help individuals manage risks and raise alarms	Wearable or smart home devices	Intruder alarms
			Alarms worn round the neck connected to a warden or control center
			Monitors of inactivity, falls, use of household equipment
			Electronic pill dispensers deliver pills at set times and raise an alarm if the pills are not taken
Preventive technologies	Predict and prevent dangerous events	Remote monitoring	"Smart" clothing contains sensors monitoring health status, e.g., heart rate, temperature
			"Tagging" devices identify patterns of movement and location
		Electronic pets	May stimulate caring responses and provide company and interest
		Remote telecare and diagnostic systems	Internet and Web/video cameras to observe symptoms

- Increased choice, safety, independence, and sense of control
- Improved quality of life
- Maintenance of ability to remain at home
- Reduced burden placed on caregivers
- Improved support for people with long-term health conditions
- Reduced accidents and falls in the home

However, Milligan (2009) points to concerns about intrusion and impersonality, for example, alarms used for some older people permit listening in or calling at the home if there is a period of lack of movement or unexpected sound, since this may reveal an accident. More intrusive still are monitors in clothing or household devices, which again may alert a control room if people cease to use their fridge or cooker or as they come in or out of the house. While such devices may be accepted because they confer a sense of security for an older person, their relatives, and official services, these are examples of potentially unwelcome intrusions into people's lives. Demand to use them may increase because they are cheap rather than for the security they offer. Also control rooms are staffed by distant, faceless people not personally known to the older person, who may resist them because there is a lack of personal contact. Although we are familiar with the kind of pet-like electronic games that children and young people find entertaining and stimulating, these and physical devices with some of the same characteristics may also be impersonal. But, for some people, it may be better than no contact with others. People may dislike the idea of remote diagnosis and treatment by doctors or nurses for similar reasons, but this may be a practical alternative, or necessary for very specialized treatment in rural or remote locations. It may also allow local or informal caregivers to receive professional advice about caring, without waiting for visits.

Integrating Social Care Services for Older People

We saw in chapter 2 that integrating services for older people is an important issue. Because most older people are self-caring or cared for by family and others in their community most of the time and, as we saw in chapter 1, may only come to require services over time, social care services are presented with a particular management difficulty. Although, like a housing welfare office, they have a base for their services, most of their services are provided in special caring environments or in people's homes. Like a hospital, they have caring accommodation, such as care homes, but this is also someone's home, rather than a place you go to for occasional, short-term treatment. And, even though they have caring staff and equipment, these also have to be delivered to people's homes. Unlike health care or social security, social care is not a total system, it has to interact with other services and with informal caregivers.

The following organizational factors are also relevant:

- Social care is multi-sectoral, being provided first by informal caregivers in families and communities, in the public sector, the private sector, by for-profit agencies, and in the voluntary, or third, sector by nonprofit agencies or charities.

■ Social care involves providing interpersonal care but in a context of also planning and commissioning services. Commissioning means authorizing a person or organization to carry out official or formal care responsibilities by establishing, planning, or financing services appropriate to social needs.

■ Social care focuses on caring provision for people with long-term conditions, so there are no brief episodes of service but rather a continuing provision, although the roles of other services, family, and community caregivers sometimes makes this intermittent service.

There are two important processes for achieving these outcomes: case management, out of which cash-for-care schemes are developing; and services for informal caregivers.

Case Management

Case or care management, or managed care (the American term), is important because in many countries it is the main way of integrating services to make them relevant for a particular individual. The case manager takes responsibility for putting together services in a "care package" tailored to the specific needs of the older person. There are two main forms of case management (Challis, 1994; Kanter, 1989):

■ Administrative case management—the case manager carries out an assessment and arranges services but does not necessarily remain in a continuing relationship with the service user

■ Clinical case management—the case manager provides a continuing supportive relationship as the services are used

Case management is based on an American model, mainly aimed to coordinate relatively fragmented services. It starts from a screening process. At first, this was intended to produce a needs assessment of the locality, to enable resource decisions to be made on a full understanding of needs in a particular area. However, in administrative case management, this aim is often degraded to become a screening of applicants to see if they meet basic criteria for service provision (Payne, 1995, 2009).

The further stages of case management form a cycle, in which an assessment is carried out, leading to a plan for the services to be provided. Then service provision takes place, which is monitored to ensure that it is working according to plan. Periodically, a review of the assessment takes place, leading, if required, to a renewed care plan. Case management is carried out by a range of professionals, including social workers.

Case management has developed in two main areas of provision:

- Management and integration of services provided to adults requiring long-term social care, often using an administrative model
- "Assertive" care management for people with mental health difficulties, a clinical model in which practitioners actively maintain contact with mental health service users who may drift if they lose touch with services, particularly if they stop taking medication (Payne, 2009, ch. 6)

Rapp and Goscha's (2004) literature review of research on effectiveness in care management suggests that effective case management involves case managers with low caseloads being in regular contact with clients and providing much of the care themselves. These research outcomes suggest a model of care management that may be successful and applicable to a range of settings. However, this kind of approach has mainly been used with the relatively small client group of severely mentally ill service users. Long-term care for other groups, such as older people, has not enjoyed a similar level of resources, and since higher levels of physical care are required than with mentally ill people, it may not be appropriate. However, elements of clinical case management could be introduced with older people, probably to their benefit.

Practice and Policy Implications

Practitioners often find that case management provision focuses on managing tight budgets, rather than exploring creatively the options for older people to develop their lives. However, looking at Rapp and Goscha's (2004) literature review may indicate some ways in which practitioners can improve the quality of their interpersonal work in an administrative model. For example, it may be possible to foster client choice and increase contact with clients for brief periods as important decisions are made.

In a study of "low-level" needs of older people, Clough et al. (2007) suggest that targeting people with the most needs may exclude people from services for low-level needs. Focusing solely on high-level needs might mean that services were less sustainable and less cost-effective. There might be a human rights argument for meeting low-level needs, but resources available may be ambiguous and shifting. The main areas of low-level help that older people needed were around the house and garden, staying in and getting out and about, managing personal affairs, staying informed, shopping, transport, socializing, leisure, and recreation. It was important to look at everyday needs and help for special occasions: for example, while shopping appears to be an everyday task, people also need to shop for birthday and Christmas presents, and this may need personal help or community projects outside the family. The sensitive practitioner thinks about both the everyday and the special.

Cash for Care

Cash-for-care schemes are a development or replacement for case management, which try to answer some of these problems. They provide payments (in Ireland, for example, called "home care grants") or vouchers (in Finland, for example, called "service vouchers") instead of case managers organizing a package of services. A study of cash-for-care schemes in four European countries found that there were four main reasons for introducing them:

- To promote choice and autonomy for older people
- To plug gaps in existing provision, where services were not available
- To create jobs
- To promote efficiency, cost savings, and domiciliary care (Timonen, Convery, & Cahill, 2006)

There were, therefore, a mix of service development and resource management aims, as with case management. These changes were slow to make an impact on services, although the intention in the UK is to make direct payments available to everyone receiving long-term social care. Similar developments in several countries suggest that this may become an important trend, particularly because there is an insufficient labor force to meet growing demand as older age groups become increasingly frail and may become socially isolated (Ungerson & Yeandle, 2007).

However, there are also many difficulties. Public services often focus on people with the most severe needs, with people with moderate needs mainly paying for their own care or being supported by their families. This kind of work is often affected by gender stereotypes, being perceived as "women's work." It has been seen primarily as domestic work and is low-paid because, for example, only contact time with service users is paid for, not travel or personal development time. Consequently, the level of skill and personal involvement is often not recognized, and female workers and family members may be exploited (Yeandle, Shipton, & Buckner, 2006). Also, there is evidence that many older people and their families do not want to take on the responsibility of managing services directly.

Services for Informal Caregivers

Among the services found useful for caregivers of older and disabled people are:

- Early identification of the need for support, since caring often wears people down
- Comprehensive medical and social assessment so that all aspects of the needs of older people and their caregivers are identified
- Timely referrals to other services as soon as problems arise
- Continuing review and responsiveness to requests for help
- Active medical assessment and treatment of the older person so that treatment needs are not missed and caregivers can receive advice about how to manage particular conditions as they arise or as symptoms change
- Information, advice, and counseling
- Regular help with household and personal care tasks
- Regular breaks from caring responsibilities, which may involve time away from the older person, or time with them with additional support so that caregivers can regain ordinary roles with the cared-for person, as spouse, social companion, and lover
- Consistent financial support and regular reassessment
- Permanent residential care, organized so that the caregiver can retain some caring responsibilities and involvement (Lewin, Sinclair, & Gorbach, 1983)

Social care systems increasingly make support for informal caregivers available. This list makes it clear that such support can be helpful at a variety of different stages in the pathway through services to aging people.

CONCLUSION

In this chapter, I have reviewed social care and social work for older people in the context of broader social provision. I have argued that the main role of social care services is to improve the quality of life of older people by providing appropriate care in an appropriate place, developing appropriate human and other resources to achieve this. The importance of place in social care for older people derives from the preference of most older people to remain self-caring in their own home, as they age from a family-building phase of their lives. Where self-caring is not possible, caring interacts with the accommodation in which older people live, and social care interacts with a range of social provision for all citizens. Social care provision for older people includes domiciliary care in people's homes, care homes, day care, and, increasingly, assistive technology.

Case management has provided a means of integrating these services, but the administrative form used in older people's services has not achieved the flexibility and creativity that might be hoped for. Cash-for-care services, developing from care management, are in many places beginning to replace or add to care management to improve outcomes by increasing older people's control of and participation in planning their own care. Services for informal caregivers from clients' families and communities are another important aspect of service integration.

FURTHER READING

Social Care Practice in Context, by Malcolm Payne (Basingstoke, UK: Palgrave Macmillan, 2009).

This book explores social care practice in the UK and provides a useful guide to implementing case management services in a caring and individualistic way.

Internet Information

One of the best government Web sites about aging and older people in the world is provided by Aged Care Australia, the Web site of the Australian Department of Health and Aging, whose title shows what an important issue aging is in that country. It provides a good account of the range of services available: http://www.agedcareaustralia.gov.au/internet/agedcare/publishing.nsf/Content/Streaming+page

The UK National Services Framework for Older People (a division of the Department of Health) provides a useful online publication, *National Service Framework for Older People* (2001), which lists of a range of services that might be available in health and social care for older people: http://www.dh.gov.uk/prod_consum_dh/groups/dh_digitalassets/@dh/@en/documents/digitalasset/dh_4071283.pdf (retrieved March 31, 2011).

The U.S. National Clearing House for Long-Term Care Information (part of the Department of Health and Human Services) provides brief, clear guides both to general principles and to the U.S. system: http://www.longtermcare.gov/LTC/Main_Site/index.aspx.

More information about informal care can be found on the Web sites and links available from organizations concerned with their role:

- Caregivers resources from the U.S. government: http://www.usa.gov/Citizen/Topics/Health/caregivers.shtml
- Carers Australia: http://www.carersaustralia.com.au
- Carers UK: http://www.carersuk.org/Home
- Eurocarers: http://www.eurocarers.org—this site has a good range of resources and links covering many European countries
- National Family Caregivers Association (NFCA): http://www.nfcacares.org

Social Work Skills with Older People

AIMS

This chapter discusses the social work skills required in providing services for older people; in the following two chapters we move on to building on these skills to practice critically and creatively.

After working through this chapter, readers should be able to:

- Think through their professional stance in working with older people by looking at "what's up?" and working in a "can do" way
- Analyze and develop appropriate professional skills in working with older people
- Empower clients' participation in thinking ahead and thinking aloud about future plans using an advance care planning process
- Incorporate the preferences of older people and their informal caregivers through assessment and care management skills to create and implement tailored packages of care for older people
- Work effectively within caring services

PROFESSIONAL STANCE

An important starting point for practitioners is to consider their stance toward their clients. We saw in chapter 1 that citizenship social work practice seeks to be holistic (Payne, 2011), including in practice a concern for the body, the mind, and the social. First, practitioners need to know about the older person's physical and mental capabilities and understand how frailties interfere (or do not interfere) with doing the things they want to do. Second, they need to understand the social context. Part of this is the life story that has led to this point and that explains what in that life is important now, and who is important. Another part is aspirations for the future and plans to achieve those aspirations or find alternatives if they cannot be achieved. The third aspect of a holistic understanding is the caregivers, family, and community who surround the older person and contribute to their capacity to achieve what they want to achieve. Citizenship practice follows the same principles but incorporates a particular concern for the rights of older people to respect, dignity, and equality.

I focus particularly on starting from the client's narrative, that is, their account of how they have come to their present situation. Incorporated in the decisions that they make in order to tell their story, older people make priority decisions about what is most important and either explicitly state or sometimes imply their explanation or reasoning for the sequence of events they describe. One of the important things about listening to a narrative in this way is that people understand and are accustomed to storytelling, whereas asking them to identify requests, issues, or priorities at the outset is not a customary way of thinking. The practitioner can extract and test their analysis of the narrative on the client to see if they have picked up the major issues. Narratives also bring forward the main people involved in their story and point to connections between them. In listening intelligently to a narrative, practitioners look for and ask about gaps in the story and the social context that they need to understand why and how things happened

Holistic practice includes a whole practitioner and an integrated service; holism does not only apply to the older person and their social context. I find it useful to think about the appropriate professional stance in two ways:

- What's up?
- Can do

"What's up?" means that the practitioner looks, through the narrative, at the long-term and recent history and identifies and checks out current issues that arise from the past. "What's up?" allows the practitioner to pull out what seems important and ask, "Is that right?" "Can do" means taking responsibility for making sure that things happen. For example, if someone asks you about something they need, you replace "Sorry, we don't do that, try . . ." with finding out and referring them to the right agency and checking that something happens as a result. If a request is reasonable for the person and their social relationships, nothing should get in the way of achieving it.

Case Example: Getting Husband and Wife Together

A man in his eighties had a stroke and was admitted to hospital for treatment, then transferred to a rehabilitation unit (a second hospital) with a plan for eventual return home. Shortly afterward, his wife was diagnosed with a relapse of her cancer, which had spread widely through her body. She was eventually admitted to a third hospital for treatment because of symptoms of renal failure caused by the cancer. While a family member who was a nurse thought that her mother was dying, the renal team proceeded with a planned operation for kidney removal. The family asked for the husband to visit his wife, but this was refused because it might lead to cross-infection, which was an issue of current public concern for the hospital. The renal team was focused on its treatment, rather than the possibility of death. The husband required a well-equipped vehicle to transfer him, so the absence of an ambulance obstructed the visit. Eventually, the rehabilitation team's social worker, helped by two assistants from the rehabilitation unit, transported the husband in a borrowed vehicle adapted for transporting people in wheelchairs, and facilitated the visit; the wife died shortly afterward. The family was pleased with this rule-breaking behavior, but their letter of thanks led to the social worker being reprimanded for causing risk to the man.

Later, concern was expressed about the excessive emotional "lability" (rapidly varying emotional expression) of the man, which was obstructing achievement of his rehabilitation target to return home. The lability was thought to be a residual symptom of the stroke and led to a psychiatric assessment. The rehabilitation unit records did not contain information about the wife's death, which was irrelevant to the rehabilitation role, and the psychiatrist was not aware of it. The possibility that the man was suffering a grief reaction became apparent at a case review with the social worker present. It was only then that the social worker was able to suggest the importance of planning for support in returning home. The team had been assuming that there would be no problems with this, while the husband was worried about returning to a home where his partner in life would no longer be present. Assistants in the unit were aware of his concerns, but this had not been passed on to the rehabilitation staff, who were mainly concerned with his improving physical capacity.

This sequence of events illustrates the importance of taking into account the full range of factors taking place in people's lives and thinking about likely emotional and social responses to them; "what's up?" asks you to think through what might be the consequences of what is happening in people's lives. It is also important to be prepared to overcome obstructions to meeting those emotional and social needs—"can do"—because other objectives will not be achieved unless factors that are more important in how people see their lives are properly resolved.

Kerr, Gordon, MacDonald, and Stalker (2005) provide a useful summary of research about social work practice with older people, starting from older people's views and then examining outcome research. They summarize t points of research as follows:

- Older people looked at the service as a whole, rather than distinguishing particular contributors to their service and focused on good relationships with the people providing services. Therefore, practitioners need to develop good relationships with older people and ensure that other people involved with their clients, such as formal caregivers, also maintain good relationships.

- Older people thought relationships were good when they were treated as individuals, capable of exercising choice and control over their lives; we saw this in the research on dignity, reviewed in chapter 1. They valued assessments that looked at the things they were able to do, not needs or problems. A holistic approach to assessment and service delivery is valued, if it is provided with sensitivity, flexibility, and respect for personal dignity. This accords with the principles of humanistic social work.

- Since older people focused on the whole service that they received, effective assessment, care planning, and review were the most important aspects of the social work role from their point of view because social work designed and integrated the whole package of service.

We see here that older people had a holistic view of their care, rather than seeing it in separate services; and their citizenship, equality, and respect were important priorities. I start with communication skills, since building an effective and respectful working alliance with older people and their informal caregivers using these skills is the most important foundation for assessment and care management. I then move to the assessment process, starting from advance care planning, which makes sure that clients' and caregivers' own aspirations and plans are up-front in the assessment. I then look at assessment processes and the practice of case management, picking up the account of this service in chapter 3. Here, I look at the practice of tailoring a package of care to the preference and needs of the older person and their caregivers. Finally, I look at social workers' contributions to effective caring services.

Most of the discussion does not explicitly deal with inequalities between minorities. However, picking up the comment in chapter 3 about the social work role of "cultural translation," an important role for practitioners is ensuring that they and other participants in networks of care, as well as staff and informal caregivers in care homes, are aware that they are caring for people who will inevitably come from different cultural locations. This includes different ethnicities, sexual orientations, and religions, in addition to experiencing the cultural dislocation of being cared for in a place whose culture is different from theirs. Citizenship practice means enacting the equality of all cultural positions.

Case Example: Mr. Fairfax's Confidences

Mr. Fairfax, newly in a care home confided to his social worker that he had heard some care workers joining in jokes among other residents about an openly gay performer on television. He did not want to emphasize that he was gay to other residents, but he had found this discomforting. The social worker discussed this with the manager, and a staff training session on appropriate responses to different sexual orientations was arranged. This revealed some prejudices; staff came to understand the importance of respecting the sexual identities of people in the care home. The manager found that this had to be periodically reinforced. He also thought to introduce staff discussions about other inequalities.

BASIC COMMUNICATION SKILLS

This development of an appropriate starting relationship with older people comes from the use of basic communication skills in practice. Lymbery (2005, pp. 140–143) emphasizes that this should include verbal skills, such as clear speaking, listening (to reassure older people that what they are saying has been heard), and, particularly with older people, nonverbal communication, such as facial expression, eye contact, appropriate physical distance, and posture. Practitioners also require good skills in writing to clients and writing about them clearly, succinctly, with respect, and without jargon in reports seeking resources for them. On the other hand, we should avoid inequalities in communication, where professional and agency agendas dominate the conversation, and a tendency to look at superficial practical problems rather than the emotional and family consequences of them.

Geldard and Geldard (2005) identify general skills for engaging people in a relationship and beginning to elicit their story, and I have adapted these as they apply to working with older people:

- Greeting and observing clients and putting them at ease; checking that they are able to see and hear you, since watching your lips may help to overcome hearing difficulties. Your name, job title, and role; your agency's role and who asked you to visit help to make connections with people that they know; and an understanding of how you fit in with the several official visitors that they might receive. I find it useful to leave a visiting card; it helps people remember who you are and how to contact you. More important, they can talk to other people about you and feel you are in contact with them, rather than being an anonymous official.

- Inviting them to talk and tuning in to their attitudes and feelings is an important starting point. Although you should initially say what the official reason is for your visit—for example, to carry out an assessment for a package of services—you should emphasize that you want to hear from them first. I find it useful sometimes to put aside ostentatiously any forms I have to fill in, look directly at the older person, and get them to talk to me. It is important to hear their narrative of events and pick up their priorities from what they tell you.

- Listening with interest, using minimal responses such as, "uh-huh," "I see," "okay," and stronger invitations to continue, such as, "and then . . . ?" It is important not to interrupt their flow, but encourage them with interest and concern.

- Expressing support and interest through nonverbal behavior, by concentrating on what they are saying and picking up your next question from something they have said.

- Speaking clearly at a suitable speed and volume and accepting silence appropriately. When clients go quiet, they are often thinking through something that they have not encountered before or managing an emotional response to something. It is important to give them time to do this, rather than pushing them on to something else; it shows them that their feelings and reactions are important to you.

- Paraphrasing content to check and demonstrate that you understand; this is an important listening skill. This does not mean repeating it, but rather putting what the person said into your own words.

- Experiencing and reflecting back your understanding of feelings that the client expresses to gain a sense of the impact of these feelings and to check that you have accurately understood how he or she felt.

- Summarizing at appropriate points your overall understanding of what clients have said. This puts the whole narrative into a context and checks that you have understood the implications and direction of their narrative.

- Closing the session comfortably with a final summary and by explaining what you will do now, what they and their caregivers may need to do, saying when you will come again, and what you will do on that occasion.

- Marshall and Tibbs (2006, p. 90) emphasize the importance of not changing your use of language when communicating with people with only mild dementia, since their communication skills are intact and they may find simplified language use patronizing. Also, avoid using a questioning approach, since this places people with a short-term memory loss at a disadvantage; instead start with a statement about who you are and why you are talking to them, and let them pick up on your statements. People with more advanced dementia may make apparently disconnected or incomplete statements, but by listening carefully, you can often see connections and test your thoughts out on the client (Marshall & Tibbs, 2006, pp. 98–99).

- Discussing bad news is a difficult area. Bad news is anything that will have an adverse impact on the older person's life or future plans, such as diagnoses of serious illnesses or dementia. A useful approach is to start by asking clients and family members to tell the story of diagnosis and treatment so far and how they see what has happened. Is there anything that they particularly fear or are worried about? There may be things that you can reassure them about, as well as situations in which you have to confirm their fears. If they seem unrealistically pessimistic, it may be useful to ask them to compare how their condition differs from a previous period. You can then move on to asking whether they have had any thoughts about plans for the future, or if any immediate action needs to be taken. From this kind of conversation, you can gauge what approach you need to take to any further information-giving; this may include arranging for a doctor, nurse, or other health-care professional to talk through information and treatment or care options, and the likely progression of an illness. Many older people may have incorrect perceptions of diagnoses because they are not aware of modern treatment or care options, but rely on experience of a previous generation's illness.

Counseling skills analyses, such as this, often ignore skills that are particularly important in social work. Lymbery (2005, pp. 144–151) identifies networking, negotiation, mediation, and administrative skills—clarifying this, I would emphasize partnership approaches to working with older people in their family and community and with other formal and informal agencies and caregivers. We have seen in chapter 3 how these contribute to integrating services. These are important because, unlike counselors who mainly work just with their client, social workers have to work with a range of other participants in an older person's life and care.

- Networking involves building, within the agency, connections with other agencies relevant to their clients' needs to agree on policies and practices to coordinate their work. We saw the importance of this skill when discussing integrating services in chapter 3. Practitioners can build on higher-level agency networks with networks connecting with practitioners in their locality. Making links locally may also identify networks that agencies should key into more generally. Agencies and practitioners should develop plans and strategies for building their networks over time and sharing them with colleagues. You can usefully develop teamwork by carrying out team projects to investigate and update information about other agencies.

- There are several models of negotiation. The well-researched psychological approach of setting an exaggerated demand and accepting reductions until a compromise is reached is not appropriate in social work, because it leads to excessive expectations among clients and to conflictual or cynical relationships with partner agencies. Instead, a strong focus on evidence drawn from effective assessment of the client and family's needs and their plans can lead to outline plans identifying acceptable and unacceptable choices. Practitioners can then adopt an advocacy approach, trying to achieve the best results for the client. Relying on this, a partnership approach with other agencies of joint exploration of options is more helpful.

- Advocacy for the client's needs and preferences is an appropriate role for social workers, since their job usually involves understanding and then representing client, family, and community needs within their agency decision-making processes. Informal representations and further evidence-gathering can lead to reconsideration. Formal appeals against agency decisions may be handled by negotiating a separate role as advocate within agency systems or getting the help of an external advocate.

Case Example: Advocacy Roles

A social worker completed an assessment which was used as the basis for an application for funding for a client to enter a care home. The agency put this to a joint panel that made decisions about cases for the whole community to ensure consistency of decision-making, and the social worker presented the client's case. Funding was not granted, and the family appealed the decision; the agency's papers, including the practitioner's assessment, were made available to an association for older people, who represented the client. At first, this agency used correspondence and telephone representation and finally took part in an appeal hearing.

Administrative skills include collecting evidence and representing clients well in assessment documents and case reports. Social workers particularly need to be able to write effective scenarios, which set out clients' needs succinctly and vividly. Budgeting and calculating the cost of care packages and working out alternatives, balancing priorities and levels of need to make decisions, and finding creative ways of obtaining resources for care packages are particularly relevant when working with older people. As with all social work, organizing practitioners' time and priorities effectively is also an important skill.

BUILDING ON SKILLS: ADVANCE CARE PLANNING, ASSESSMENT, AND CASE MANAGEMENT

Advance Care Planning

Advance care planning (ACP) is the starting point of assessment and case management. It is the process of finding out and recording people's wishes for how they want to be cared for or treated in the future, building on their narratives of the development of their present situation. It protects people's freedom of decision-making through openness, particularly about difficult issues that some people try to avoid. The Scottish government has introduced anticipatory care planning (Delivery and Support Team, 2010) as part of its case management initiative. It is the same as ACP, but focused on people with long-term conditions. It sees ACP as a way of improving coordination between different professions and services because it works from a single holistic statement prepared with client involvement to guide proactive, planned, and coordinated care management. By anticipating the various choices to be made through working out the likely care pathway (see box 2.2), practitioners can more easily achieve the client's preferences when those choices come up. This allows proactive planning because, when a decision needs to be made, there is a history of discussion with clients and caregivers about the direction of travel. In this way, ACP shifts social work practice away from problem-solving and toward thoughtful ways of arranging for and providing long-term care.

The advance or anticipatory care plan involves, first of all, thinking ahead, rather than reacting to immediate problems, and thinking aloud, so that problems are shared. However, the reality is that many practitioners do not get called in until there are problems to be sorted out. In this situation, ACP takes place after the initial reaction to problems, so that unexpected crises are less likely to recur. The ACP is "a dynamic record that should be developed over time through an evolving conversation, collaborative interactions, and shared decision-making. It is a summary of Thinking Ahead discussions between the person, those close to them, and the practitioner. The ACP is a record of the preferred actions, interventions, and responses that care providers should make following a clinical deterioration or a crisis in the person's care or support. It should be reviewed and updated as the condition or the personal circumstances change and different things take priority" (Delivery and Support Team, 2010, p. 1).

Henry and Seymour's (2008) guide to ACP focuses on older people and makes an important point: "The difference between ACP and planning more generally is that the process of ACP is to make clear a person's wishes and will usually take place in the context of an anticipated deterioration in the individual's condition in the future, with attendant loss of capacity to make decisions and/or ability to communicate wishes to others" (p. 3).

The Scottish government's advice develops the idea of triggers that should cause a practitioner to think about doing ACP. Triggers arise in three main ways:

- When there is a major change in clients' situations, for example, when an older person becomes housebound long-term, receives a complex care package, is in a care home, is unexpectedly admitted to hospital, frequently calls on services out of hours, or where there is caregiver stress.

- When clients' physical or mental conditions are serious, for example, when they have an advanced long-term condition, are receiving enhanced support from a specialist nurse, are using a memory clinic, or are registered as having special needs.

- When medical assessment suggests that clients' physical or mental conditions are unstable or deteriorating, when clients are vulnerable because of changes in their health or psychological state, when their caregiver's situations are difficult, when they are receiving polypharmacy (more than six medicines), or when they have had falls.

Gallagher and Ireland's (2008) research study of a Scottish project to provide ACP for a time-limited period to help older people over an immediate crisis and put in place a plan for future care was well evaluated by older people and their caregivers.

Older people's capacity to make their own decisions about their care may vary over time. Also, it may take a good deal of effort to elicit their views about their care, so it is important to start early and take time to get and record their views. Some groups, such as older people with intellectual disabilities or mental illness, may be stigmatized because professionals or their family think they do not have the capacity to think through and plan their lives. However, by repeating discussions, practitioners can build information about their preferences. They often have well-formed views about their care, but people often fail to ask or take notice of what they say. People with disabilities may also suffer from others' assumptions that their disability means that they cannot have a good quality of life, and plans for positive options are given less importance than they would be for other adults (U.S. Department of Health and Human Services, 2008).

ACP focuses on clients' preferences, not on practitioners' professional assessments and decision-making. A process that separates clients' ACP from professional records or assessment is important because practitioners' decisions focus on needs according to legislation or the agency's priorities. Talking with clients about what they want is a crucial part of any professional assessment, but practitioners' own judgments about needs color the outcomes. Many people are not accustomed to thinking about the kind of issues that arise in ACP.

One way of grounding the process is to start with people's actual experience. Have they experienced other people having a good or difficult experience? What could have been done better or differently? Then you can ask about current care needs and any values or preferences that affect their views about it, future health, or future care needs. Finally, you can ask about planning decisions in the future by asking who should contribute to decisions about care needs in the future or who might make those decisions for people. This open approach is important because it starts from clients' perceptions of their situation, that is, from their narrative. Also, it enables practitioners to discover if there are fears that come from a parent or spouse who has had a difficult experience in the past.

Assessment

The process of building up a relationship through interpersonal skills and developing a view of clients' and informal caregivers' preferences often moves into, or forms part of, some kind of assessment process. Assessment is often used confusingly to refer to different things:

- A social work assessment as part of the process of developing social work or caring interventions or therapeutic or other objectives
- A comprehensive, professional, or multiprofessional assessment by or on behalf of many different professionals who may be making a contribution to the client's care
- An initial assessment or screening to see if a client presents concerns that should trigger more complex assessments for services
- A risk assessment to decide the extent to which clients or others may need safeguarding from difficulty or danger

- A needs assessment of eligibility or suitability for a service or provision of a package of services
- A financial assessment to decide the extent of any financial contribution that a client should pay toward the cost of a service (extended from Payne, 1995)

Assessment of needs is an important professional responsibility, and practitioners have a duty to carry it out comprehensively so that full evidence and information is available to inform decision-making. Comprehensive assessment also gives clients and caregivers confidence that all their circumstances have been considered. In the same way, we would separate the informal caregiver's wishes and needs from those of the client.

Expressing views clearly means that clients' and caregivers' preferences are more transparent, and practitioners can take people through understanding what is on offer and get their informed consent to receiving these services, even if sometimes they are not completely satisfied. The practitioner can then help them to appreciate why they cannot have what they want and direct them toward any appeals process that is available. This enhances both justice and clients' security that practitioners are looking after their interests.

Drawing on a range of research, McDonald (2010) identifies the following main components of assessment that practitioners should focus on:

- Strengths—what clients can do and achieve, rather than what they cannot do and their problems
- Citizenship—maintaining clients' engagement in social networks and in planning and managing their lives
- Autonomy—maintaining clients' control of their lives and decision-making that affects them
- Information—making sure that clients and their families have access to information about any problems and sources of help
- Personal development—identifying ways in which clients can continue to learn and develop personal skills and interests

Wright et al. (2005) devised a "social difficulties scale" to explore problems experienced by routine cancer patients; it involves asking about difficulties in a series of areas where problems often arise for older people. This is inappropriate for citizenship practice because it focuses on the details of the negatives, and the scale is only validated for cancer patients. However, the research identified three clusters of sustained issues in the lives of patients: physical ability, providing for the family, and contact with others. Looking at these areas offers a useful guide to our focus on balancing social issues with physical abilities. Practitioners should be asking about how clients are able to provide for their own and families' living needs, and with whom they have contact. Ecomaps, described below, offer a visual format that helps to do this.

Case management systems (see chapter 3) are increasingly using universal assessment procedures and IT to aid data collection and decision-making. Egan et al.'s (2009) Canadian study of decisions found that case managers used a mixture of clinical expertise combined with being a broker using local information. This gave them flexibility in using nonstandardized interviews and overrode system directives when they led to misleading results. The UK Single Assessment Process (SAP) for adults is an example of such procedures that aim to promote working together by enabling all agencies to contribute to a joint assessment, avoiding the need to ask repeatedly for the same information. Research has suggested that achieving such cooperation is difficult, because of incompatible computer systems and lack of trust between different professionals. McDonald (2010, p. 63), reporting these findings, suggests that such systems also rely on expert questioning approaches, using assessment tools or precoded questionnaires. Such an approach does not engage with the situations as seen by older people and their families.

Case Example: A Disabled Woman and Her Grandchildren

A visiting nurse on behalf of a medical practice asked for a social work assessment of Mrs. O'Neill, who had increasingly severe Parkinson's disease but was caring for the three preschool children of her youngest daughter. The nurse felt that Mrs. O'Neill experienced an unreasonable degree of stress because of this but had been unable to persuade her that she should give this up. The nurse was concerned that she had an unrealistic view of her increasing disability and was also worried about the safety and proper care of the children. The social worker used a narrative approach to hear Mrs. O'Neill's story, which was of a very difficult daughter with a history of drug abuse, living in another town, rejected by her other children. Mrs. O'Neill was in despair about having to care for the children but also wanted to support her daughter to make progress in life. The social worker was able to work with a colleague in children's services to assist the daughter to achieve better child care arrangements.

However, the SAP documentation does set out an account of the areas that assessment might usefully cover, which accords with the practice in many social work agencies across the world. The brief notes required for the record can rely on the narrative that practitioners have already discussed and provide a useful way of checking the accuracy of the practitioner's understanding. I have added to this account humanistic approaches that focus on strengths rather than problems:

- A brief account of presenting problems or needs. The humanistic, strengths-based approach outlines positives in people's lives and is particularly cautious about accepting definitions of problems from referrers or family members, who may assess issues from the point of view of family demands or agency or professional interests.

- Relevant personal history. While practitioners will avoid collecting unnecessary information, enabling older people and their families to set out a narrative of how they have arrived at this point allows them to present themselves as independent and competent persons who have tried to overcome difficulties, disclosing strengths that will contribute positives to any future plans. It also places present problems in a social context.

- Cultural, spiritual, and personal issues relevant to the assessment. This refers to experiences and values that show what is important in people's lives. While this may be a formal faith or life objectives, it may also include important relationships, important interests, leisure pursuits, and personal development objectives.

- Informal support and formal care services received and the contribution that they make in the perception of the older person and the family. The assessment allows practitioners to value a contribution already made and see how a willingness to help can be integrated with formal services. It is important to make clear that present contributions to caring will be neither rejected nor assumed to mean that no formal services are needed.

- Important domains of assessment, including physical and psychological well-being, activities of daily living and how these are achieved, social relationships, family members, and informal caregivers. It is important not to make clients feel that relationships they have developed in another context, such as work, social clubs, or church, must be converted to informal caring; people should be able to keep some relationships separate from their caring needs.

- Caregivers' needs and concerns. Recognizing these and finding ways of offering support will strengthen family relationships, help to integrate formal with informal care, and maintain relationships for the benefit for the older person. Failing to recognize them may lead to caregivers feeling excluded from engagement with the practitioner and formal services. They may then try to carry on without formal help, thus adding to the demands on them.

- A brief statement bringing together and providing a summary of relevant factors, painting a word picture of the important aspects of an older person's life and the care they receive.

- Formal decisions about care needs, which may be the basis of administrative decisions about charges and the level of services that can be provided.

VISUAL REPRESENTATIONS OF ASSESSMENT

A number of techniques allow you to represent information visually. I describe three here. The most common is genograms. These focus mainly on family relationships because they were created to show genetic connections between people. However, you can add nonfamily relationships or even pets. Social workers also sometimes use ecomaps to present wider social connections and network diagrams to display links with services. Spiritual ecomaps identify connections that are spiritually important for clients.

Genograms or Family Trees

Genograms were devised for studying genetics, but the complex symbols used for that purpose do not have to be transferred to social work practice. Box 4.1 shows a sample genogram with some common symbols; practitioners can draw these readily, and they give a good picture of the main family relationships. Additional information or notes on the importance of particular relationships may be added—for example, pets, nonfamily friends, and lodgers. Because we are working with an older person in this example and patterns of illness in the family are not particularly relevant, the genogram starts with the client's generation.

PAUSE AND REFLECT: Thinking through a Genogram

The example shows how making a genogram permits the practitioner to discuss relationships and may immediately raise questions that may affect practice. Looking at the example in box 4.1, what issues would you want to discuss?

Some Suggestions

Emily's current relationship with Fred and other current partner relationships in life may be issues for her long-term support; just because they are divorced does not mean that they do not support each other or live together. Sue and Pete were not legitimate children of Emily's first partnership: will this affect their

Box 4.1 Example of a Genogram

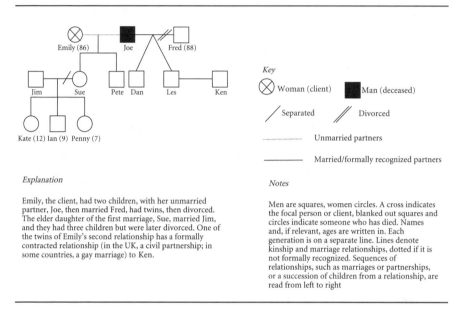

Key

⊗ Woman (client)   ■ Man (deceased)

╱ Separated   ╱╱ Divorced

⋯⋯⋯ Unmarried partners

——— Married/formally recognized partners

Explanation

Emily, the client, had two children, with her unmarried partner, Joe, then married Fred, had twins, then divorced. The elder daughter of the first marriage, Sue, married Jim, and they had three children but were later divorced. One of the twins of Emily's second relationship has a formally contracted relationship (in the UK, a civil partnership; in some countries, a gay marriage) to Ken.

Notes

Men are squares, women circles. A cross indicates the focal person or client, blanked out squares and circles indicate someone who has died. Names and, if relevant, ages are written in. Each generation is on a separate line. Lines denote kinship and marriage relationships, dotted if it is not formally recognized. Sequences of relationships, such as marriages or partnerships, or a succession of children from a relationship, are read from left to right

entitlement to inherit money from Emily or attitudes among other people? For example, the children of Fred's marriage may oppose their involvement with family support. However, Sue has the only children in the family: What is their relationship with Emily? Will there be bereavement issues for them at the end of life, or are other more distantly related children close to Emily? What are attitudes in the family to the gay relationship between Les and Ken? Because this is formally contracted, it will be public knowledge, and there may be conflicts in the family about it.

Ecomaps

Ecomaps offer a picture of the relationships and support that are relevant to an older person. They start from a genogram and show links outside the family. The example in box 4.2 describes three different sorts of relationship, connected with two people in a marriage—there would often be more.

This is drawn on a standard format, but ecomaps may also be drawn freehand in the record if this is more convenient. The format can be adapted, and the second example shows an adaptation by Hodge and Williams (2002) to show important spiritual relationships, simplified from a more complex format in Hodge (2000). Here the standard questions lead to discussion about any faith in a god, involvement in organized religion, rituals used, which might not involve

Box 4.2 Ecomaps

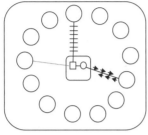

Standard format—clock face; each circle is an important relationship

Key

Dotted line—weak relationship

Crossed line—strained relationship

Arrowed line—strong relationship

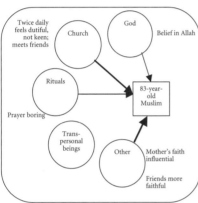

Adapted format—Hodge's (2002) spiritual ecomap; each circle is a standard element of spiritual assessment; line thickness shows strength of commitment

Key

God—belief in a deity

Church—involvement in formal religious worship

Rituals—interest in rituals such as meditation

Transpersonal beings—direct experience of more-than-human forces outside self

Other—additional factors related to religious belief

formal religion; for example, behaviors such as meditation and other matters relevant to religious belief. "Transpersonal beings" refers to spiritual forces influencing the person's life; for example, some Christians have visions of angels and some people refer to fate or luck.

Agencies or practitioners can adapt ecomaps to provide standard formats like this to inform their work.

Network Diagrams

Box 4.3 shows a network diagram used by an agency as a standardized reminder of the links that an old person might have. Starting from their home (residents are listed, and in the boxes above, information such as main leisure activities at home and transport available may be noted), you can draw lines to contacts for leisure activities (the smileys at the top of the page), health care (the crosses on the right), other agencies involved (the boxes at the bottom), family members (houses on the left in the nearest column), and friends (houses on the left in the

Box 4.3 Network Diagrams Help to Identify the Structure of People's Lives

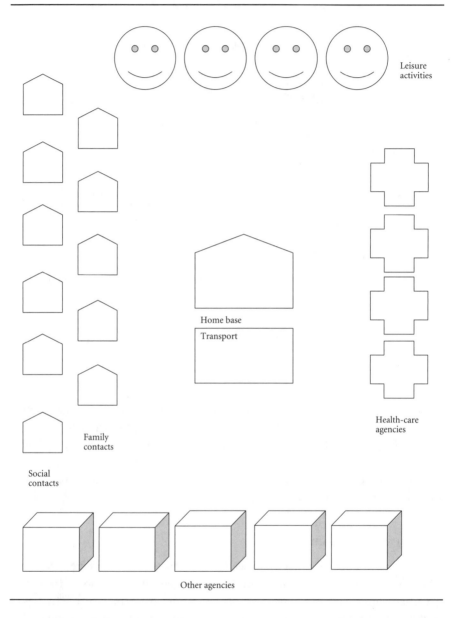

furthest column). Arrows on the lines show whether the older person visits or the contact visits, or both. Means of transport and length of journey can be noted on the lines. This can give the whole picture of an older person's social network at a glance.

SOCIAL WORK ROLES IN SOCIAL CARING SERVICES

The basic social work skills discussed above and the important social work role of assessment contribute to packaging services that provide social care for older people. However, these important roles should also lead to action to help clients and families. Lymbery et al.'s (2007) research study of British social workers identifies three main social work roles; these are typical of social work in many countries:

- Assessment for and organization of services. This is the main function required of social workers by services for older people in many countries. Although assessment is mainly a beginning point of case management, simply exploring an older person's life and relationships can be helpful in helping them think through what they want for the future and can appropriately be connected with advance care planning (ACP). Sometimes, moving further into case management is not needed, since with this thinking through, the family can deal with many of the issues without further intervention.
- Helping older people with the emotional and practical impact of transitions as they age. Social workers in this study thought that greater attention to this role would be socially useful and valued by clients, but paying attention to such interventions was restricted by the time taken up in the assessment role. This is why I argue for the value of incorporating some interpersonal helping with the assessment role.
- Dealing with discrimination and risk occurring because of aging. The social work profession often carries an important responsibility in this area; for example, where families are not caring for or responding appropriately to the needs of older people. I deal with these issues in chapter 8.

Once the assessment is carried out, social workers have to intervene. What skills can we use to develop practice in this wider range of activities? Geldard and Geldard (2005) set out the general skills involved in helping people, and again I have adapted this list to practice with older people:

- Confronting clients respectfully when they are avoiding important issues. For example, if they say they have no problems, we can ask them to compare the things they can do now with an earlier period, or say specifically what they would like to be able to do but cannot.
- Normalizing by helping clients understand where their behavior and reactions are appropriate to their situation. Anxiety about physical or

mental frailties can be assessed by looking realistically at what the client can still achieve and at new possibilities to replace now impossible activities.

- Reframing stories or experiences so that clients and services can see them differently.
- Challenging and changing destructive beliefs, drawing on techniques from cognitive behavioral therapy. For example, one or two increasing disabilities do not mean that all aspects of the personality are going to go downhill.
- Helping clients to identify situations in which they hide important emotions or other aspects of their situations. An example is where they hold back from telling caregivers about their preferences or something that has upset them for fear of losing support.
- Helping clients identify and make use of their strengths, focusing on things that clients can do, rather than things they can't. (Mr. Calman, in the case example that follows, is an example of this.)
- Focusing on the here and now to see what we can change. Clients may not be able to get back to full independence, but they could attempt some more things than they are doing now. How can we find help to support them? (Again, Mr. Calman is an example.)
- Exploring options for change. There may be more alternatives than just staying at home or going into a care home. Options may include day care or treatment for a particular problem that increases the alternatives available.
- Helping people take action through encouragement and influencing their environment. For example, are there things that could make it easier for you to do what you want to do?

Case Example: Mr. Calman's Falls

Mr. Calman had a number of falls, leading in one case to a broken arm, due to increasing arthritis making him unsteady when he carried things around his apartment. The social worker who was his case manager had an anxious meeting with Mr. Calman and his daughter about whether he was so much at risk that he needed to think about admission to a care home; he was resistant to this. The social worker asked them to talk about what had happened. Mr. Calman mentioned woodwork items and tools to pursue a hobby. He was making wooden toys for his grandchildren and for charities in the area. He had previously been able to use a local workshop where he had been employed, but being unable to go out, he had given this up, and although he had tools, he did not have equipment to hold the objects he was working on securely. The social worker suggested that they should focus on how he could pursue his activities, rather than on what care he needed, and eventually was able to arrange for Mr. Calman to go to a day center that had equipment, but not expertise, that could be used for woodworking. Mr. Calman was able to advise and support other day center members in doing woodworking tasks, attending three days a week. At the same time, he agreed with his daughter and the social worker on some sensible precautions about how he should move around at home, and some additional changes were made to his apartment to assist with this. Here the risks were confronted, but by listening to and reframing what was going on, alternative arrangements avoiding a care home were made.

How can we apply these general ideas to working with older people? There are a number of factors:

- Being in the category of "older person" implies that the client or other people perceive a change or separation from a past life. Therefore, it is particularly important in practice to help older people and the people around them make the connections with their past life and its potentialities. Reminiscence is a practice technique that focuses on this element of practice.

- The future for older people may be limited, and people may see them as "in God's waiting room," at the end of life, having no valuable life left. It is particularly important to look for positive achievements or fulfilling activities, planned according to the time that people realistically may have left. Creative activities and practice are important in this aspect of practice.

- Older people's intentions and plans may be limited by frailty, ill health, and changes in their lives, but bringing their own plans to fruition enables them to retain control over what is happening to them. Therefore, planning and service provision need to focus specifically on their own intentions and wishes.

Reminiscence

Not everybody values reminiscence. Coleman's (1986) study of reminiscence as part of adjusting to aging identifies a number of different attitudes:

- Valuing memories—these were people who regularly looked back on their lives and valued their memories.

- Regret and resolution—these people looked back on their lives with regret about things that had happened or things they had done but found resolution in thinking them through and accepting the bad with the good.
- No point in looking back—this group represented a variety of attitudes. Some had adjusted to their life and dissatisfactions with it, and chose "not to go there"; others focused on the present—"keeping going" was the priority.
- Loss and depression—a small group did reminisce but felt that a disappointing life had led to loss.

Coleman suggests therefore that practitioners need to be prepared for and support a range of reactions to the idea of looking back on life. They may also need to support people with disappointment and loss, perhaps helping them to see fortunate aspects of their experience. I look at reminiscence again in chapter 7, since it is often done in groups.

RESIDENTIAL CARE

Residential care practice in care homes or nursing homes is sometimes not seen as a social work skill, but practitioners are often involved with older people entering care homes and with supporting them and their families and informal caregivers while they are there. Much of the practice can be transferred to other settings, such as day care. Citizenship practice points toward what Clough (2000) calls "resident-centered" care. This starts from a focus in practice on developing understanding of the preferences and wishes of residents as a basis for making positive relationships with them so that they feel they are at the center of decisions about how the home runs. The care home should seek to develop a daily life and routine that meets those needs through the relationships that practitioners and caring staff establish. That routine should include time to listen to and build relationships with residents. Practitioners and staff in the home should negotiate actively with residents about how things are organized, and residents should feel that the focus of staff's efforts is meeting their needs.

Brown Wilson (2009) distinguishes three types of relationships in residential care for older people:

- Pragmatic relationships between staff, residents, and families—getting the job done
- Personal and responsive relationships between residents, staff, and to a lesser extent families—finding out what matters to the resident

- Reciprocal relationships that take into account the communal nature of living within a care home—developing a shared understanding of how we all fit in together

Being able to achieve this depended on the layout and structure of the home, continuity of staff, leadership, staff's personal philosophy, and the contributions of residents and families. Burton (1998) sees holistic residential care as bringing the resources of the residents' skills, time, and interests together with staff, the place, the residents' money, and the service's finances in a planned way to achieve the appropriate care in an appropriate place. We often see this as being about making a residential care home "homey." But one person's homey is another person's untidy, and while homey may be appropriate for a resident's personal space, it may not be appropriate for an entrance hall or the manager's office.

PAUSE AND REFLECT: Places Appropriate to Relationships

Think about the relationships that will be carried out in a resident's personal room, communal lounge, kitchen, bathroom, office, and group room in a care home for older people. Reflect on the relationships that will take place in those settings and how the environment should be established to reflect that.

Some Suggestions
The resident's personal room might well contain many personal possessions but should not be so overcrowded as to be unsafe, remembering the practical care that may have to be given. There should be provision for privacy so that residents can have secrets from visitors and staff. The kitchen will have to reflect its working role, be hygienic, and be efficient. However, it may also be a favored place for informal interaction between kitchen staff, residents, and other staff; perhaps a suitable environment in one part should be set aside for this.

The main roles for social workers are:

- Finding ways of involving older people in decisions about the kind of care that they want, helping them formulate and implement their advance care plans.
- Helping to build regular links with older people's contacts in the community or in their social networks. By exploring their social networks, using ecomaps or network diagrams of their past lives and present possibilities, or listening to narratives of their experience, practitioners may be able to encourage better contacts with family and friends.

- Maintaining contacts with other services that might be useful to the older person.
- Identifying additional services that might give greater interest and flexibility in the older person's life. Building on skills and experiences to develop creative work and groupwork are important aspects of this (see chapters 6 and 7).

Behavior as Communication

Social workers may well be consulted or asked to intervene about behavior ("Mrs. Jones is being difficult") and relationships between residents, families, and staff. Behavior communicates thinking, so if an older person is crying a lot, they may be worried or depressed about something; if they flinch when you are helping them, they may have a painful joint; if they eat in a strange way, they may have mouth problems. Therefore, keeping an observant watch on changes in behavior can help you to understand what an older person is thinking or feeling. Staff members who consult about behavior should be asked about changes and any known factors in changes.

Careful observation of behavior can also identify trigger points. Is Mrs. Jones flustered or difficult around mealtimes or bedtimes? Perhaps some relaxation or a premeal or bedtime drink may help. Sometimes it is not surprising that older people are worried, frightened, or angry if they have experienced changes to their routine or are living in a new place. If they express anger or distress, it is important to stop and allow them to express this; it will help to identify what the particular problem is and with the effort to make adjustments. At least it may mean that they can express their anger or distress appropriately and not upset relatives or other residents.

Wandering and Walking

Wandering and walking is often an issue for older people with dementia, particularly in hospitals and care homes, and there is a fear that this may lead to accidents or injury, with people getting lost in the neighborhood and causing worry to neighbors and others. Marshall and Tibbs (2006, pp. 99–100) point out that if clients are physically well, they are unlikely to give up a lifetime of walking. Also, going out relieves boredom, stimulates interest, and permits people to make choices about their physical position and view. Therefore, discouraging sitting in one place, having a range of activities, and making available spaces such as safe gardens (see chapter 6 on a "dementia garden") can limit these problems. It may also be useful to take people out with staff in pairs or small groups to sit in a local park or walk to local shops. Some supported housing and care homes specializing in dementia do not prevent residents from walking around but have staff available to go with them or shadow them, bringing them back when they are ready; this is often feasible because not every resident decides to walk around at once, and after periods of activity, people will often stay in one place for a while.

Case Example: The Concert

Mrs. Knowles seemed distressed and ran out of a concert in a care home; other residents were concerned. A care assistant went after her and walked with her to her room. She found out the one particular song had provoked unhappy memories. A comforting drink and a talk about other songs Mrs. Knowles remembered reduced the distress.

Case Example: Dressing Mrs. Kennedy

Mrs. Kennedy had arthritic joints and disliked being dressed in the morning. The care assistant formed a pattern of doing one thing at a time, then talking briefly about some happy memories; occasionally they sang a favorite song together. It took a bit longer but was less distressing and built their relationship.

CONCLUSION

This chapter reviewed social work skills in working with older people. The main emphasis was on how to interpret and develop basic professional social work skills for working with older people. Using advance care planning (ACP) and assessment are important ways of facilitating older people to make decisions about their future and their care and enable them to review their needs. A citizenship approach to social worker includes these professional, empowering functions within the social work role that is established by the case management systems with their service integration aims discussed in chapter 3. Understanding older people's attitudes and preferences is an important aspect of helping them to maintain their individuality and quality of life as they change the place in which they live during the last phases of their lives.

FURTHER READING

There are a number of books on social work with older people. This listing is of books published in English since 2005 which, while they draw on the particular nation of publication, have very broad coverage of social work professional responsibilities.

Foundations of Social Work in the Field of Aging: A Competency-based Approach, by R. R. Greene, H. L. Cohen, and C. M. Galambus (Washington, DC: NASW Press, 2007).

Older People, Aging, and Social Work: Knowledge for Practice, by M. Hughes and K. Heycox (Crows Nest, Australia: Allen and Unwin 2010).

Social Work with Older People: Context, Policy, and Practice, by M. Lymbery (London: Sage, 2005).

Social Work with Older People, by A. McDonald (Cambridge, UK: Polity, 2010).

Social Work with Older People (4th ed.), by J. Phillips, M. Ray, and M. Marshall (Basingstoke, UK: Palgrave Macmillan, 2006).

Working with Older People, by D. Tanner and J. Harris (London: Routledge, 2008).

All of these provide useful practice guidance on working with older people.

Focused Genograms: Intergenerational Assessment of Individuals, Couples, and Families, by R. DeMaria, G. Weeks, and L. Hof (Philadelphia: Brunner/Mazel, 1999).

This text is useful if you want a detailed and comprehensive guide to using genograms.

Internet Information

A useful range of practical and academic resources is available on the SCIE dementia gateway: http://www.scie.org.uk/publications/dementia/index.asp.

Critical Practice with Older People

AIMS

The main aim of this chapter is to review the application of critical social work to practice with older people.

After working through this chapter, readers will be able to:

- Understand different areas of critical social work
- Identify how critical social work ideas may be used in practice with older people
- Recognize how critical social work can renew practice with older people

CRITICAL SOCIAL WORK

Critical social work is a range of ideas for creating freedom in and through social work practice, for both practitioners and older citizens. The next sections examine in turn two important aspects of critical practice that we can apply to social work with older people:

- Critical thinking—not taking for granted commonplace assumptions about what we are dealing with or how we should work. This helps to free us from limitations created by our own and others' assumptions about social work with older people.
- Critical practice—using theories that question the existing social order to guide practice actions. Existing care systems are part of a society that limits the opportunities and outcomes of social care for older people. Critical practice helps to free us from those limitations. Our practice aims instead to empower older people's self-actualization by

providing social relationships and services that offer a good quality of life. Critical practice also seeks to create social change that affirms the citizenship of older people in society.

Critical Thinking

Critical thinking offers three main techniques:

- Critical analysis of language. This involves thinking carefully about how you communicate with an older person or their family members. For example, do you ask too many questions? This might make them feel they are answering a barrage of points that you are in control of. A more narrative approach helps clients retain control of the order and style of communication.
- Avoiding taken-for-granted assumptions in practice. This involves a questioning stance about the accepted norms of your service. See below for more on this.
- Critical discourse analysis. This is a technique for deconstructing, that is, taking apart, discussions and disagreements between people or between social institutions to identify power relations between them. For example, if an older woman seems very rejecting of her daughter's reasonable suggestions to offer help, what do they argue about? Perhaps it is about the older person's privacy in her home; or perhaps there is a relationship history of attempts to control the mother.

Case Example: A Son Is Overcontrolling with His Mother

A doctor asked a social worker to visit because he felt a son, the main caregiver of his mother with a progressive neurological condition, was being very controlling. The social worker assumed that the son was concerned about his mother falling or injuring herself, but a conversation on this basis came to nothing. Then, the social worker stepped back a bit and asked them both to tell the story of their life together. This showed that the mother and son had both been physically abused by a very violent husband/father, from whom after many years they had escaped. During this period they had formed a very close relationship in which they looked after each other. The mother accepted the son's domination because of their mutually dependent history. The social worker was able, using cognitive behavioral techniques, to help both of them see that their joint behavior was unhelpful to them both. The approach was to train the son to try every week to list actions that gave his mother freedom to do something on her own. After a couple of weeks, the son got the hang of this, and his mother was easily able to negotiate greater freedom for herself.

Critical Thinking in Practice with Older People

Adams, Dominelli, and Payne (2009) suggest several helpful critical thinking strategies that we can use in practice. First, they point to the importance of complexity thinking. As a starting point, practitioners can try "and/also" rather than "and/or." This means searching for ways of including several aspects of an issue rather than focusing on dualities. Practitioners should not say, "If we do this, we cannot do that," but, "How can we incorporate both of these issues and others besides?" This connects with the idea of discourse. Instead of seeing the issues that a client faces as a debate between two possibilities, we should rise above the debate and look for overriding issues that offer alternatives or new opportunities to develop a new narrative of people's lives. Similarly, reflexivity offers a new way of looking at issues. It involves taking inside and outside views of a situation: the easiest approach to this is to start from different descriptions of the same event or situation and then progress to how different views about how people feel about it can be incorporated into our intervention. Finally, examine how you feel about how your client says he or she feels about the situation.

Case Example: Fruit at Lunch

Casey was a senior care assistant in a care home who was asked to respond to a complaint from a relative of a new resident. The complaint was that the resident did not like the fancy cream-filled cakes served for dessert at lunchtimes and would prefer to have fruit, which would be healthier. Casey prepared a reply, which explained that cakes were liked by many residents, and there were insufficient staff to prepare and serve individual menus. She then discussed it with the resident's social worker, who knew the relative well. The social worker came to watch lunch being served and discovered that this was the only dessert served each day; the supper was usually a snack meal only. The social worker commented that perhaps care staff in the home were feeling that they must defend the reasonableness of their practice. It was also possible to take the approach that a suggestion for an individual highlighted a possible alternative for everyone. Staff could think over possibilities. Getting the care staff and cook together, the social worker commented that residents ate at tables grouped in fours, some of whom needed to be fed. It had been planned so that no more than two residents at each table needed to be fed, so that staff were not clustered round a few of the small tables. The social worker wondered if there were alternative ways of doing this, while thinking about the suggestion. The group came up with some possibilities and eventually developed a plan. Instead of each resident being served an individual plate, two choices, one involving fruit, would be supplied to each table; if one table ran out of a particular choice, they could swap with another table—this offered some resident control. Where residents could serve and feed themselves, they could take their preference; where they needed help with serving (some residents) and eating (more), it would be easy for staff to serve another resident from the choice and then move to help with eating. Using this system, residents had a wider choice, and it was discovered that some who had been fed cakes were able to spear pieces of fruit, so they no longer needed feeding. When the choice was made available, more residents chose fruit when they liked the fruit offered (and reverted to cake when it was better in their view).

Eventually, residents asked for a larger selection of fruit, which two residents with lap tables on their wheelchairs carried round the tables at both lunch and supper for people to pick from, and the cooks came up with a way of chopping fruit so that it did not become a slushy fruit salad, which the residents also said they disliked. Casey was able to write back to the relative that, as result of her suggestion, a new system had been introduced for all residents and that this had introduced wider choice. She already knew this, but it was nice to get a formal acknowledgment of the contribution her suggestion had made. In addition, the residents enjoyed the swapping and self-service elements of these developments, probably because it gave them a sense of greater control and choice in their lives. The staff also knew far more about their residents' preferences and could drop unfavored cakes and increase well-liked fruit.

This is an example of treating residents like citizens rather than as dependent care-receivers. Adams et al. (2009) identify practical critical thinking that is focused more on how services are organized. They suggest that practitioners should try to contextualize issues that arise, thinking through how policies and organizational structures have affected the situation. They should also try to problematize issues that are taken for granted. This helps to free debate, which may identify nooks in a policy or set of practices where alternatives are possible. It is also important to be self-critical, to think how the agency or the practitioner may be a part of the problem. Finally, it is important to try to identify barriers or social divisions that are creating the problem and may be at least modified and perhaps removed.

Case Example: Volunteers in an Assisted Housing Scheme

A large assisted housing scheme had, in addition to a number of staff, a group of volunteers that had been set up about ten years before when the scheme had opened initially as a care home; other less intensive elements had been added later. The volunteers had set up their own association to provide their services, and this had received charitable donations. Many of the volunteers preferred visiting individual residents in their rooms or apartments, and there was a shift system for this work. A few volunteers organized craft activities in the communal lounges in the scheme. The groups were long-established and produced goods for sale as part of fund-raising events held by the scheme, raising money so that residents could go on visits and to improve the environment. Recently, there had been a larger than usual turnover of residents in the scheme, and most new members did not want visitors, did not want to take part in the groups, and preferred that the funds raised be spent on improving the scheme's facilities rather than group visits to local events, in which many residents were unable to participate. These points were made individually to staff, who eventually reported them back to the committee. Several members of the committee felt that the new generation of residents were ungrateful and that staff had devalued the work of volunteers. A local social work manager was asked to help out in this conflict situation.

She talked with a range of people involved. In reporting back, her approach was to suggest that the structure of the volunteering scheme, set up to achieve financial assistance, was now not helping new residents to participate in the assisted living scheme and that, by working jointly with residents, the volunteers would be able to achieve new purposes. She pointed out that at the outset, the facilities were brand new, but now a lot of renewal would be beneficial, for example, providing communal Internet facilities, which several of the residents would like.

This led to several more resignations, but a small group of remaining volunteers reconstituted the association, at her suggestion, as a planning committee for a new support scheme. Her analysis was that the volunteer scheme was now mainly benefiting the volunteers' self-esteem rather than residents' needs. Participation and engagement in decision-making was the way to achieve the change. The social work manager was able to help the remaining volunteers to reconstitute the association with residents having a 51 percent majority on the committee, a symbol of their ownership of it. Accumulated money was spent on an Internet café, which provided Internet access and support in using computers for e-mail and mobile telephones, which many of the residents now possessed. Two of the volunteers became helpers at this facility, and another converted themselves to a practical financial adviser assisting residents with completing welfare and other forms that residents were finding difficult. After a while, the committee found that some of their practical visits were also moving on into personal advice and support over personal issues. Residents had disliked regular volunteer visits when they had no choice of who visited them. Some craft groups continued, but newly designed cards printed on the computer array also joined the fund-raising products, and a residents' Internet blog started.

PAUSE AND REFLECT: Review Critical Thinking

Go through these two case examples and identify how they illustrate the elements of critical thinking listed.

Some Suggestions

In the assisted homes scheme example, the structure of the volunteer group and their consequent power over the way their help was organized had become a barrier to change, and the response to this focused on giving residents more power. Both examples increase social justice for client groups involved, giving them greater power and reducing their unequal status in the situation. In the care home meals example, the social worker thought in terms of "and/also"—how can we offer both types of dessert?—focusing on everyone's choice rather than how they could justify a limitation in one person's choices.

CRITICAL PRACTICE FOCUSES

Critical practice contains a number of different, sometimes conflicting, ideas. I divide them into three groups, elements of which sometimes overlap:

- Political and social policy focuses are about the social values expressed in how care services are organized. They emphasize social change through political and policy change to achieve social justice.
- Social work aims focuses emphasize the need to change social work so that its aims concentrate on reducing inequalities and oppression in relationships.
- Gerontological focuses are an example of applying values, policy, and practice to the particular needs of older people; another example might be critical mental health perspectives.

Political and Social Policy Focuses

Critical political ideas in social work draw on neo-Marxist political philosophy to propose that social work is an aspect of the economic, political, and cultural domination of oppressed groups. As part of state- and non-state-organized social welfare systems, social work expresses political philosophies that are contrary to the interests of clients. Critical social policy ideas analyze the increasing instability of the state as a provider of welfare.

One aspect of the policy critique is the suggestion that there is no stable settlement in social policy (Clark et al., 2004). I commented in chapter 1 on the changing social settlement for older people: the suggestion of this policy critique is that there will be no new stable settlement. This is because economic and political globalization means that countries are no longer fully in control of their economy. Consequently, they cannot decide to have high levels of welfare provision, even if politically this would be accepted, because the costs would be unsustainably high for their economy. In transition countries in eastern Europe, such as Poland, for example, there cannot be a shift from a communist regime to a new settlement; rather there will be continual change. In African countries, economic development cannot easily go alongside high levels of social support for older people, again because the economy will not support high welfare expenditures alongside economic development, however desirable this would be. These trends push every country toward high levels of economic growth, rather than permitting a choice of welfare regimes.

The governance of welfare systems is also changing. For example, much social policy about older people focuses on the provision of state services, and much of the debate explored in previous chapters has been about how increased services for an older population can be sustained by a declining working population. Faced with such scenarios, management of welfare regimes focuses on doing more for less, that is, providing increased service at lower cost. Social care governance tries to manage high expectations, improving quality in a context of declining financial support. Every participant in governance faces conflicts. For example, practitioners must balance good interpersonal support against providing services for as many people as possible. Informal caregivers must balance their desire to help their family with protecting themselves against unreasonable stress or overwork. Uninvolved members of the public must balance their desire for good public services with their wish to reduce taxation to maintain their own economic security. So informal caregivers may be engaged in governance mechanisms with conflicting aims. On the one hand, they may be recruited to use their experience to be a powerful voice driving up the responsiveness and quality of the service by professionals. On the other hand, by engaging them in service provision, they can better understand and perhaps become more accepting of the conflicts and difficulties in providing a good service. In this way, they may be led to accept the unacceptable in service provision.

A risk-averse attitude in services that comes from a legal duty of care for vulnerable people may press public services to intervene, reducing older people's freedom to live a preferred lifestyle. Risk-averse attitudes are a cultural characteristic of developed societies. However, when working with older people, they may arise from medicalization of our thinking about older people's lifestyles, leading to a concern about risk of falls or health consequences of social behavior. They may also stem from ageist assumptions about older people as incompetent or dependent.

Featherstone and Hepworth (1989) suggested three important issues for older people that arise from a postmodern perspective on aging. One is the importance in postmodern societies of cultivating a lifestyle and the development of consumerism. This may exclude older people who do not accept these values as part of their life. On the other hand, adopting a consumerist lifestyle may help to keep them feeling young and involved in current cultural values. Or, alternatively, it may press older people to make inappropriate demands on themselves, for example, in fitness and social engagement, which may prove to be a social pressure. An emphasis on the importance of youth in cultural activities that older people use, such as television, may make them feel excluded or inadequate. For example, their favorite music may not be used. Another factor is the emergence of new social movements focused on issues such as the new role of women, racism, and climate change. These may exclude concern for older people in favor of future change and may also make older people's experience seem irrelevant to issues that are important in everyday debate.

Case Example: Maya's Music and Mobile Phone

Maya was a paid caregiver for Mrs. Kinross, visiting most days to help her with personal hygiene, medication, bathing, and other practical caring tasks. While helping with personal tasks, Maya turned off her portable sound system, but otherwise she listened through earphones all the time to Caribbean music. Mrs. Kinross could hear this, as it leaked out from the earphones. Maya also received regular calls from friends on her mobile phone, which she kept switched on to receive calls from her supervisor. A visiting social worker, observing all this, talked to Maya on her lunch break. She used a critical thinking technique, reflexivity. She asked Maya to talk about how she would feel if she were disabled and had a visitor from a different culture providing physical care for her. Maya could connect with these ideas, because she herself would have been very upset if, when she was older, her daughters could not care for her and she had a paid caregiver. The social worker then asked Maya how she would feel if a caregiver listened to unfamiliar music and made phone calls about her private affairs, cutting her off from contact. She suggested that Maya could talk to Mrs. Kinross about some of her friends and play some of her music to Mrs. Kinross. A few weeks later, she had to go back when Mrs. Kinross's daughter complained about Maya irritating her mother. She helped Maya to negotiate with Mrs. Kinross about the amount of involvement she had in Maya's life. In this way, Mrs. Kinross was put back in control of the relationship with her caregiver and of the environment in her home.

Social Work Practice Focuses

From neo-Marxist political ideas, critical social work says that practice should, if possible, avoid participating in that domination and should try to combat it to create alternative empowering social structures and relationships. In particular, anti-oppression ideas emphasize the importance of combating the political and social oppression of minority client groups. Another strand of thinking is the concern for the oppressiveness of management and organizational structures in social care. From feminist and social construction ideas, critical social work takes an emphasis on valuing the individuality and emotional and social integrity of clients and others involved in social care, a concern for the development and actualization of their personal identity. These ideas are sometimes in conflict with Marxist or materialist ideas, which emphasize that social structures control individuals and questions whether individual flexibilities are freedoms or are enforced by cultural assumptions. However, both have influenced practice by demanding a democratic equality in relationships between practitioners and clients.

Case Example: Family, Service, and Social Worker

Mrs. Handley was referred by her son for home care services to support her in living at home. The family doctor mentioned a number of incidents that suggested she was in the early stages of dementia, although she would not go for a formal medical assessment. The social worker visited to assess her for social care services and found that Mrs. Handley was managing quite well. It became apparent in discussions that both the doctor and the son felt that it was inappropriate for the son as a male in full-time employment to take time from his work to provide personal care and wanted to establish a (female, although they did not say this because it was taken for granted) caregiver in preparation for difficult times in the future. The social worker agreed to build up a relationship with Mrs. Handley over time by offering membership of a local social club, which increased Mrs. Handley's social network.

In this case, the social worker identified gender and medicalizing assumptions about the future course that were influencing the doctor and the son. She reacted by moving toward some personal development actions for Mrs. Handley and an improved relationship.

Gerontological Focuses

These ideas use the critical gerontology explored in chapter 1 as the basis for proposals about the aims and organization of services and social work practice with older people. Looking at who dominates or controls older people's lives, gender and other potentially discriminatory assumptions, trends toward medicalization, and political concerns about economic and managerialist assumptions about how services should develop are central here.

PAUSE AND REFLECT: Thinking Critically about Critical Practice Focuses

We can bring the two aspects of critical social work together and apply them to work with older people. Reflect on the following case example.

Case Example: Mrs. Brady's Worries

Mrs. Brady was in hospital for a treatment for kidney failure. In the early stages, a doctor visited her bedside, physically examined her, asked a lot of detailed questions about her physical problems, and set up a treatment regime, answering Mrs. Brady's questions about her condition and treatment. Nurses perceived afterward that she seemed anxious and asked a social worker to talk to her. The social worker started her conversation by following the approach in chapter 4, saying, "What's the main thing on your mind at the moment?" This led to a conversation about Mrs. Brady's grandparent responsibilities for the children of her working daughter, who could not afford to give up work to care for her children. The social worker talked about how important grandparents were in many people's social arrangements, and they talked about how they could set up a shift of other family members to help. Part of the issue was how long Mrs. Brady would need to stay in hospital and whether this was an uninterrupted period or Mrs. Brady could spend some time at home. The social worker called the doctor back, and they had a three-way conversation about possibilities for community treatment. It was finally agreed that, if this went well, most of the treatment after the first two weeks could be done on an outpatient basis. It seemed that the daughter could work shifts in the evenings and weekends for a while, and Mrs. Brady could resume a lot of caring responsibilities. Talking with the doctor afterward, the social worker told him how valuable it had been to be able to talk through the various possibilities for treatment; it had not occurred to him that this was relevant to his task, but having heard Mrs. Brady speaking raised his consciousness about the social consequences of medical treatment decisions.

Stepping through the critical thinking and critical social work practice focuses discussed above, can you identify how they arose in this case example and how the social worker tried to deal with them?

Some Suggestions

The doctor not unreasonably used a diagnostic and treatment planning approach, asking questions to achieve the objectives set by his treatment responsibilities. The social worker's citizenship narrative approach was more democratic and allowed Mrs. Brady's concerns to lead her work. The social worker did not accept the taken-for-granted assumption that the hospital was there to treat Mrs. Brady's condition. She modified this by focusing on treatment within the context of important social roles in Mrs. Brady's life. She deconstructed the doctor-patient conversation by seeing that while treatment aims were shared—Mrs. Brady wanted the treatment—the doctor had not extended his view to wider social and gender roles as a grandparent caregiver, which were just as important to Mrs. Brady, so their conversation had not been complete. This is an example of the medicalization of a service, focusing on medical priorities to the exclusion of other concerns. The social worker also used "and/also." She did not see the medical treatment or the grandparent roles as alternatives, but planned to include them both and find compromises that allowed them both more equal importance. In turn, this respected the important roles of older people as contributors to society, rather than emphasizing older people as the objects of care and treatment.

IMPLEMENTING CRITICAL PRACTICE

Alternatives and Opportunities

Critical practice, therefore, involves seeking alternatives in service provision and practice that enhance social justice and equality for older people as part of practicing social work. It seeks to develop positive alternatives to enrich people's lives, rather than seeing care services as dealing with people who are problems. Critical reflection is a technique for individual practitioners to test their practice against critical practice objectives on enhancing social justice. It has developed strongly in recent years (Fook & Gardner, 2007; White, Fook, & Gardner, 2006). It aims particularly to focus on the sense of powerlessness that comes over both clients and practitioners in the face of established processes and organizational priorities. Working by first unsettling present assumptions, it then allows a more flexible analysis of the situations, enlarging the possibilities that might be open to a practitioner and client. Using the narrative approach to reveal the process by which people have reached an impasse, it allows a recasting or "re-storying" of events, so that a new option may be taken forward. If clients' situations are complex or the result of a long process, it may be useful to try to identify critical incidents—particular events that had a strong influence on creating the present situation. Possible alternatives at those points may help to identify changes that could be reintroduced now.

PAUSE AND REFLECT: See Case Examples as Critical Reflection

Look back over the case examples in this chapter and identify instances of critical reflection.

Some Suggestions

In many of these situations, people felt themselves to be powerless to respond, but listening openly to what was going on in these situations opened up freedoms and opportunities and reduced the sometimes unthinkingly oppressive use of power on behalf of organizations or professional responsibilities. By listening to the clients' narratives with the overly controlling son, the worker was able to identify potential uncertainties in their future lives that were having an impact on their present and needed to be respected. The social worker looking at residents' meals and the manager's critical analysis of volunteering in the assisted home scheme gave the residents greater control as citizens through participation in how they were supported. The social worker gave both Maya and Mrs. Kinross some control back over their relationship. Mrs. Handley's social worker focused on gender power relationships as a critical factor in deconstructing the reasons for the referral. Mrs. Brady's social worker reasserted the power of the client over the treatment decision, providing the opportunity for other alternatives to come forward.

Ray, Bernard, and Phillips (2009) suggest focusing on a number of issues that would combine both the policy and practice aspects:

- The content of assessments and methods for making them. For example, assessment might focus on enhancing what people can do rather than defining what they cannot do as criteria for a managerialist practice that concentrates on justifying eligibility decisions.
- Questioning the ideology underlying services and decisions. For example, do they see older people as valuable citizens with a contribution to make to society and able to develop their personal identity and skills or as people at the end of life who require the most economic forms of care to reduce their dependence on the state and the working population?
- Paying attention to the detail of different views of the situation. This facilitates critical thinking. For example, conflicts between older people and family caregivers may not reflect cantankerous behavior in the older person or abuse by the caregiver but long-standing family conflicts.
- Contextualizing evidence by understanding theoretical and value positions. We use ideas about the instability of state responsibilities for social care, changes in the financing and governance of social care, the pressure to develop consumerist lifestyles, and new social movements that emphasize environmentalism and gender and health

equalities to put decisions about older people in context. Is risk-averse policy treating older people as unsafe and requiring intervention instead of offering reasonable freedoms?

- Helping others understand an overview of the situation. Health-care professionals often focus individualistically only on their patient and their responsibilities; a broader view can achieve a more flexible response.
- Making sure all involved understand the perspective and the content of the service. For example, is its main focus medical, rather than examining the broader needs of older people?

Phillips, Ray, and Marshall (2006) suggest that one of the important ways of avoiding risk-averse organizational practices is to focus on the idea of uncertainty, both in the long term and short term. Similarly, Reith and Payne (2009) suggest that social work at the end of life needs to balance "truth and hope"— that is, the realities of the situation that an older person may be facing with maintaining motivation. These ideas call on us to explore with people the opportunities in their situations alongside the losses and risks.

Case Example: Mrs. Oliver's New Life

Georgina was a social worker supervising a bereavement service volunteer who was seeing a woman in her seventies, Mrs. Oliver, whose husband had recently died after suffering from a progressive disability for many years. Much of the early conversation between the volunteer and Mrs. Oliver was about loss: her distress at her husband's death and the closeness they had achieved during the long period in which she was his main caregiver. Mrs. Oliver seemed to be unable to think about balancing these understandable feelings with a restoration focus on renewing her life. She talked about suicide "to be with my husband." Georgina suggested that the volunteer should work with Mrs. Oliver to think through new activities she could build up. They did a network analysis to think about her contacts. Also, the volunteer might ask about some of the difficulties of caring for her husband for such a long period. No new positive directions emerged from these discussions, although Mrs. Oliver began to acknowledge the stresses of being a long-term caregiver. Unusually for a woman, she appeared not to have many links with other friends, and other family members lived at a considerable distance. Finally, toward the end of her period of work with the volunteer, she talked about another informal caregiver she had met at a local group for caregivers, and it emerged that she had had a sexual relationship with this man. Moreover, his wife had also recently died, and he was pressing her to reestablish their relationship. This had raised her guilt about the relationship while her husband was still alive. Georgina encouraged the volunteer to talk about Mrs. Oliver's uncertainties; there was hope that this could be a new life, but fear that it might be damaged by her guilt at the past sexual relationship. Toward the end of her sessions, Mrs. Oliver formed the view that she would maintain the contact and see whether her feelings developed toward a future relationship, rather than looking back at the past "indiscretions," as she put it.

Mrs. Oliver's case draws attention to the importance, when looking at opportunities, of recognizing the uncertainties of people's lives and difficulties in pursuing opportunities. Opportunity work needs to go alongside reality work.

Issues and Aims

Three important issues in current care systems (Milligan, 2009) can help us to identify appropriate aims for critical practice:

- Porosity—to what extent can older people gain access to care systems, find their way through the various pathways among services, and move from one aspect of the service to the next?
- Integration—to what extent can older people gain care that integrates the provisions of the four sectors of the economy (public, private, for-profit, and voluntary nonprofit and informal care) and different professional specialties and informal care?
- Extitution—to what extent is it possible for older people to remain outside institutional care or to leave care institutions if they are admitted to them?

Responding to porosity directs our practice to three areas that will help older people gain access to services: knowing what is available, providing understandable information about it, and helping people to access it. Genuine access means helping people to understand how a service might help them in their situation, bearing in mind their personal identity. For example, an older person who was born and brought up in an area may feel differently about a service than someone who is new to it; each would need an appropriate approach to building their confidence that this would be the service for them. The service also needs to respond to their needs. Perhaps an apparently well-off older person in rural housing will need free transport to take up a day center place, whereas an apparently poorer person in the inner city can make it without needing transport help, but may need help with warmer clothing.

When older people reach the assessment stage of service provision, it is more empowering to help older people and their families understand the criteria for service and present how they meet them. Practitioners can base their presentation of applications and advocacy within the service decision-making process on clients' own efforts at self-presentation.

It may also help both porosity and integration if older people and their families understand a typical pathway through the service and the services likely to be available and how they fit together. They may not have to accept or apply for every element at once but can begin their care pathway without understanding the full complexities. Planning for later developments can be done in advance or staged throughout the client's care career.

It is also important to plan to reduce the need to use more intensive forms of care that involve institutionalization. This should lead us to see admitting people to care homes as a positive choice rather than a last resort (Wagner, 1988). It can only be made a positive choice, however, if practitioners offer worthwhile alternatives:

- A positive and equalizing relationship, which facilitates older people and their families in using services, thus increasing porosity
- Challenging a focus on health care rather than social networks, family and community relationships, and creative personal development and self-actualization
- Providing good information to enable both older people and their caregivers to express their preferences and make choices
- Balancing risks that an older person faces with their rights
- Balancing the preferences of an older person against the preferences and needs of informal caregivers, ensuring that both aspects of service are adequately provided for
- When there are problems, and change is required, focusing on the older person's preferences and well-being, rather than limiting the options to available services and safety-first approaches
- Recognizing the diversity of ways of living through aging processes and supporting continuity with past preferences and self-actualization

Looking at social work with dementia, for example, Jones (2008) identifies a shift away from the medical model and an emphasis on the individual experience and personal and social identity that comes from postmodern critical thinking and social construction ideas. They emphasize anti-oppressive practice that focuses on the effect of structural oppression in society, problems of bureaucracy, managerialism in society counterposed with creativity, balancing users' and caregivers' interests, and the problems of dealing with risk and change.

The concern about medicalization and excessive focus on health care is an important aspect of many critical analyses of services for older people. However, social work practitioners are often part of health-care agencies and work closely with doctors and other health-care professionals. Moreover, we noted in chapter 1 that it is important not to neglect health-care issues in people's lives, which can improve people's quality of life, if they are resolved. Social workers can usefully develop a strategy for dealing with their engagement in health care by making clear the value of their alternative perspective by:

- Demonstrating their contribution to health-care priorities through providing education, assessment, and helping with issues that health-care professionals often find difficult, such as relating to families and communities
- Providing evidence about the importance of social priorities in the lives of patients
- Being explicit in how they integrate research and other knowledge from social science perspectives into their practice
- Identifying how social work removes barriers to people accepting and using health-care provision
- Identifying how they can enhance the service by working on social issues and social relationships in older people's lives

However, seeking to de-medicalize situations does not mean ignoring the importance of health-care issues, which may reduce older people's control over their lives. Polypharmacy—taking several different medications—may be an important issue for social workers to grapple with, especially when people suffer from dementia. Most older people suffer from several different conditions for which medication may be prescribed, often by different doctors in different specialties. The combination of drugs or simply the overall load of medication may be affecting the client's functioning.

CONCLUSION

This chapter has sought to provide a positive additional perspective on social work practice, drawing on critical ideas to meet the aim of developing a citizenship social work practice. In addition to the role of ensuring appropriate packages of service provision examined in chapter 3 and using social work skills explored in chapter 4, citizenship practice requires the incorporation of critical ideas in practice. I have argued that this can be done through critical thinking techniques and a critical practice approach that introduces into practice interventions awareness of important social conflicts about aging and the social position of older people. With that awareness a central part of our practice, we can then go on to reduce the everyday impact of inequalities and instabilities in social provision for older people.

A further step is needed: citizenship practice must also develop creative opportunities in practice and use group and macro approaches. These aspects of citizenship practice are explored in chapters 6 and 7.

FURTHER READING

Critical Issues in Social Work with Older People, by M. Ray, M. Bernard, and J. Phillips (Basingstoke, UK: Palgrave Macmillan, 2009).

This book explicitly develops a practice based on critical gerontology.

Critical Reflection in Health and Social Care, edited by S. White, J. Fook, and F. Gardner (Maidenhead, UK: Open University Press, 2006).

Practicing Critical Reflection: A Resource Handbook, by J. Fook and F. Gardner (Maidenhead, UK: Open University Press, 2007).

These two outstanding books offer a firm basis for using critical reflection in practice.

Internet Information

The Internet journals *Critical Social Work* and *Social Work and Society* allow you to keep in contact with critical ideas: http://www.uwindsor.ca/criticalsocial work and http://www.socwork.net.

Creative Practice with Older People

AIMS

This chapter develops the importance of flexibility and creativity as an aspect of practice and explores how techniques drawn from biographical, narrative, and arts therapies can be used to enhance social work practice with older people.

After working through this chapter, readers should be able to:

- Develop creativity in their own practice
- Evaluate the importance of creative work as part of their practice
- Identify ways of incorporating creativity in everyday practice
- Consider ways of using life review as part of their practice

CREATIVITY IN PRACTICE

Citizenship practice says that, as citizens, older people are entitled to practitioners' best efforts. Since every older citizen will have a different life experience and be facing a different social situation, flexibility in our responses to their preferences and interests and those of their informal caregivers is needed. In chapters 3 and 4, I argued that creativity in practice and in the development of services was a crucial element in being able to respond to older people's preferences for the kinds of services they would prefer and the way in which they would want them provided. In chapter 5, I argued that creativity emerges partly from criticality. If practitioners constantly review their own thinking and the assumptions on which they work, they give themselves opportunities to be more creative in their practice.

The reason why this is an issue in work with older people is the history of seeing practice with this group as concerned with the provision of services, or practical rather than emotional care. Trends over many years have led toward seeing social care practice as a technical task that can be managed through sets of procedures rather than requiring judgment and discretion from practitioners. This reduces complex decisions carried out in interpersonal relationships with clients to a series of determinations of eligibility assessed according to formal criteria. These in turn are constrained by economic limits: the unavailability of funds for providing services. The assumption, therefore, is that practitioners' first role is to say no rather than "can do," a principle of practice I introduced in chapter 4.

I argued in chapter 2 that dignity emerges from the enhancement of self-respect and personal identity. Practitioners can contribute to that through how they perceive and act toward people—through the relationships they have with clients. Enabling older people to have and increase their control over their lives is an important way of achieving that self-respect. Part of that is being able to contribute to their family, community, and to the development of their own identity as an interesting, worthwhile person. This connects closely to their continuing to be able to live their lives successfully and creatively in old age.

Creative practice focuses on a trusting relationship, rather than taking a risk-based approach. Practitioners and informal caregivers sometimes show that they are anxious or cautious about things that may go wrong. However, giving full and clear information and guidance, and standing prepared to help while the older person builds confidence in their own capabilities, can bring dividends. For example, a Swedish study of thirteen women at serious risk of being injured if they fell because they had fragile bones (Hallrup, Albertsson, Bengtsson Tops, Dahlberg, & Grahn, 2009) showed that the risk meant that they often experienced a narrowing life space. Their advanced age, physical injury, and the need for precautions led to a changed self-perception; they felt insecure. The way out of this for them was to try to maintain mobility and daily life routines. The chance to maintain social contacts through exercise activity was valued. Examples of activities that they liked were: exercise groups, opportunities to go out walking safely, physical games, and dancing. They appreciated information and support in that it helped them to maintain their own chosen lifestyles, so clear and detailed information about what was safe and unsafe and guidance about ways that they could protect themselves while still enjoying exercise was useful. They valued trust-based care, that is, concern expressed in ways that helped to maintain their independence and trusted them to be careful. This needed to respond to their personal preferences and about activities that they liked, especially if such activities helped them to maintain a positive body image. A trusting approach helped them to accept that they could use walking aids.

Case Example: Daniel's Garden

Daniel was in his nineties and enjoyed regular activities such as growing vegetables and flowers over many years. After he had some falls at home following hip and knee replacements, his daughter became anxious about further falls in the garden of his home and tried to prevent him from continuing with his gardening hobby by taking over tasks from him. However, it was working in the garden that he enjoyed, rather than simply tasting the results of their plot of land. A social worker walked round the garden with them both, and they jointly identified areas of the garden (for example, there were low walls as the pathway turned) where there was a risk and other areas where, even if Daniel did fall, he would fall on soft ground. They worked out tasks that Daniel could easily undertake and found ways that he could do some of them sitting down; his daughter would help him move round the garden, but he would actually undertake the gardening tasks. This proved a satisfactory arrangement, and after a while Daniel also said to his daughter that looking at where there might be dangers and doing things jointly had made him feel more secure than previously. The arrangement also removed a source of conflict and increased the amount of time that father and daughter spent together on mainly non-caring activities. They told the social worker that they could enjoy something mainly social together, while she was also helping to keep him safe.

CREATIVE WORK IN PRACTICE

The Practitioner in Creative Work

If you do not see yourself as creative and artistic and do not have qualifications and experience in this field, how can you incorporate creative work in your practice?

The first answer to that question is to get rid of that assumption about yourself. Do you listen to music, read novels, watch television and films, enjoy a lovely rural or urban scene, like gardening, like to wrap presents attractively? Then you enjoy the arts and creative activity. What you may mean is that you were told that you were tone deaf or were no good at art in school—many people were. You may also think that to be artistic is some genius-level thing that only a few people have the talent for. Yes, if you want to win the Nobel prize for literature. But you chose to be a social worker, and you're probably talented at that, even though you don't expect to win the world prize for social work (there isn't one—perhaps someone should invent it). Lots of people make good livings in the arts or enjoy and appreciate doing a bit without needing to be a genius.

PAUSE AND REFLECT: Your Creative Skills

Having read the previous paragraph, list things that are artistic and creative that you enjoy and appreciate as a spectator; then things that you would like to do that you have been told you're not talented at; then things that you were okay at but never developed; then any of those that perhaps you would like to develop in the future.

Some Suggestions

I enjoy lots of artistic and creative things as a viewer; I'm a bit ham-fisted at the practicalities. Over the years I've enjoyed a bit of amateur acting and music, helped by professionals, and I've learned that you have to work and think just as hard about what you're doing and why at those things as you do in your work life. For a while I pursued ballroom dancing, took lessons, did the exams; I wasn't brilliant, but I enjoyed it, felt a sense of achievement at climbing the ladder of exams, and got fitter. I met a lot of older people doing the same.

The second answer to the "I'm not creative" assumption is that you don't have to be good at it yourself to be enthusiastic and encouraging to others. The third answer is that you are not an expert in equipment for disabled people, nursing, or medicine, but you need to know enough to refer people appropriately and to make sure services are delivered by the appropriate professionals. You can refer for and deliver appropriate creative and artistic help as well.

A Creative Arts Service

The main reason for considering the creative arts as part of services for older people is an educational one. If we want to enable older people to reach the highest possible level of self-actualization, we need to provide services that facilitate their further education. Withnail (2010, pp. 6–7) reviews the main ideas that lie behind older people continuing with learning activities and personal development, suggesting that all are relevant to education for older people:

- An emancipation or social justice model, which proposes that everyone has rights to continuing personal development
- A democratic citizenship model, which argues that citizens have a responsibility to maintain their engagement with learning opportunities
- A human capital model, which suggests that citizens have a responsibility to maintain their economic productivity and develop their contribution to society

A mix of all these models is appropriate for older people. As citizens they are entitled to maintain their personal development, and they are responsible for making a contribution as a spectator and active person in cultural matters. Interest and commitment from citizens enable creativity and cultural development to grow in societies. Creativity is a habit and a social matter. To develop creativity, people have to take part in it regularly and engage with others in doing so. Research studies of care homes show that activity or occupation is an important aspect of quality of life in care homes (Mozley et al., 2004, pp. 190–191).

Four main reasons for including creative arts in the overall service are:

1. Art and creative work is a vital human activity (Shaw, 1999), integral to a good quality of life and therefore appropriate as an element in a service that seeks to provide such a good quality of life for older people. McLoughlin (1997, p. 9) also expresses this objective in saying that the main purpose of a creative writing group in a day center is "to promote enjoyment of literature" and in another account "to help patients discover what themes and images are important to them."

2. Art and creative work enhances social interaction and a sense of fulfillment because people can see an enjoyable result from something they have achieved. Also, they are able to talk about their creative activity with others, so it gives people who may be socially isolated a topic of conversation and a way of engaging with people in their circle (see case example, "George and Eleanor's Visits," below).

3. Art and creative work can be a diversion from depression or difficulty.

4. The arts may also be a therapy (Aldridge, 1998), as a creative process that enables therapeutic interactions to take place, enabling people to develop strengths to manage difficult aspects of their lives.

Case Example: George and Eleanor's Visits

George, aged eighty-three, was engaged by a community artist working in his care home in using a digital camera, processing the images using a laptop computer, and producing images of the streets of his home town. His daughter, Eleanor, visited regularly and told care workers that George seemed like a new man. Previously, she had told him her family news, but otherwise they had only talked about television programs on her visits. Now he could talk about the things he had learned and the places that he had included in his photography as attractive or important places in his home town that younger people had not noticed. He could occasionally give her framed prints of his work—he learned simple framing, as well. She could display these at home for him to see and be proud of when he visited; he gave something to her as well as being tended to by her. She found visiting much easier, and even her teenage children were more prepared to visit George and interact with him when he visited their home.

To sum these points up, if social work with older people is about enabling clients to live life to the full, then that life will include the creative arts and they are a useful resource for practitioners wanting to engage with and develop the lives of older people.

A comprehensive arts service in care services for older people might include:

- Arts therapies. These use trained arts therapists in one-to-one or group interactions. The interactions use engagement with a piece of artwork done by the client for psychotherapeutic purposes to disclose or work with psychological or emotional difficulties.
- Arts facilitation. This uses experienced or professional artists and craftspeople to assist individuals and groups to develop their skills and achieve artistic output.
- Community arts. This aims to use shared artistic activities to strengthen the resilience and solidarity of communities, such as the residents of a care home or a community organization.

To develop artwork, is it useful to:

- Offer a choice of activities and materials so that there is variety, thus avoiding repetition and boredom
- Help people share experiences and support each other through working together creatively and helping each other
- Join shared projects
- Exhibit and enable people to give art objects created through their work to friends and family
- Encourage talk about people's responses, feelings, and motivation in working creatively
- Gain feedback to inform the service of what works, what helps, and what hinders

Creative activity can contribute to a sense of community in some communal settings, such as care homes; communication; shared activity; and the development of interpersonal relationships. Worthwhile personal relationships in an area of older people's lives that is not around "therapy" can be achieved through creative work. It can also provide a focus for settings such as care homes and day centers, increasing interpersonal contact and reducing boredom and unstimulating inactivity. Since it generates activity that can build up interest, it may reduce pressures on staff to make all the engagements fit residents and attenders.

All these processes must be carefully managed. A clear understanding of the objectives that any particular arts service aims to meet is a crucial part of providing an effective arts service. Connected to that understanding, management decisions can be made about the selection of services. Managing the service will require the setting up of appropriate management and supervision arrangements and using human resources, artists, volunteers, and other staff, appropriately to achieve those outcomes. Another important management task is articulating a vision of the contribution of the arts in any particular service and connecting it forcefully with the objectives of the overall service (Hartley & Payne, 2008).

Some Creative Arts

Practitioners and managers might consider a range of creative arts. This would include crafts, drama, literature-based work, horticulture, music, and visual arts. Both doing and viewing is possible in all cases. For example, clients might visit each other's gardens, work at potting and tending plants in a day center or care home, visit well-known gardens, or listen to talks and demonstrations about particular specialties, such as bonsai or cacti. You can get examples of what might be possible by walking round an art or craft store; you can get even more examples by walking round a superstore or looking at a craft supermarket on the Internet.

As an example of the range of possibilities, music interventions may be active, in which clients make music as individuals or in groups; or receptive, in which clients listen to or experience music. People who are deaf may experience music through vibration. Musical experiences may be tailored, that is, planned to meet particular social or other needs. Tailored musical experiences include:

- Listening to music
- Performing music on an instrument
- Improvising music
- Composing music
- Using music combined with other creative activities, such as movement, imagery, or art (Bradt & Dileo, 2010)

Case Example: A Community Music Group for Older People with Dementia
Quinn, Heathcote, Hong, and Plummer (2005) described a music group in day care for older people with dementia in a rural area. As well as craft and lunch periods, the group is founded around music. A single drumbeat called people from a beginning social event to participate. Involvement in playing percussion instruments and movement to the percussion follows. Later, music is used as the basis of a reminiscence group.

USING ORDINARY ACTIVITIES CREATIVELY

Most people do not think of their everyday activities as creative; however, they can be made creative. This section suggests some examples of how we can do this. I have purposely selected examples that people can carry on if they are housebound or limited in mobility.

PAUSE AND REFLECT: Ordinary Activities Redesigned Creatively

List some ordinary daily activities for yourself, your parents' generation, or older people who are clients or in a care home. How could these be more creative? How could creative activities be attached to them?

Some Suggestions
The overall approach is to do something active about an everyday activity in which we are normally passive. To achieve this people might keep a diary, notes, or a record of what they have done. More up-to-date, it is fairly easy to set up a blog or Web site in which we can present the diary for other people. To achieve this, practitioners can encourage clients to select one aspect of the event or activity that they are recording that particularly connects with them. They could also select an issue to be critical about: they might be encouraged to rant about something they have seen on television, for example.

For a personal or more public diary or log to be creative, it needs to specialize, to concentrate on particular topics, or to have features that are special to the person who is making it, so that it is individual and more interesting. This follows the principle that activities that are affirming for older people who may be excluded from their past social life should be identity-creating. Many of the creative activities described here are identity-creating because they involve keeping records of a family or community past.

Another important element of being creative is to do something that can be taken on, that allows further progress toward greater self-fulfillment. Having been critical about something in a personal diary or blog, anyone can contribute criticism or comment to Web sites on the Internet. For example, people might be able to comment on local issues on the local newspaper or television station Web sites, on film and TV actors, and celebrities often have fan clubs or personal Web sites where criticism and comment can be submitted. There are also many discussion Web sites on specialist topics.

For many older people, involvement with computing or Internet activities may seem challenging because they do not have experience of new technology. As time goes on, increasingly this will not be so. Even where it is, simply familiarizing oneself with a new way of doing something is creative.

Learning from and criticizing television seems passive but can easily be made creative. Older people watch television a lot of the time as a form of relaxation, without using creative faculties and without actively engaging with it. Ways in which this might be achieved are:

- Plan viewing to see something new every day.
- Identify one new thing learned from each program watched.
- Identify one actor in a drama or commentator on sports or news that the viewer especially likes or dislikes and make a list of the reasons why this is and reasons for the opposite view that they have not previously considered.
- Taking things on might involve finding out more about the topic they have learned about, putting their thoughts into a diary, then a blog, then onto public comment Web sites, or writing a letter to a newspaper.

Doing something new is another good way to be creative. People can try the following possibilities:

- Do one new or out-of-the ordinary thing each day—for example, a new recipe, a new flavor or type of drink, or a new sandwich filling.
- Do something you usually do in a new way—walk on the lawn in bare feet, dress or comb your hair with your eyes closed.
- Greet someone you have not met before each day. My mother used to stand at the front door when she was housebound and do this—often it led to a conversation, usually brief, with someone new, but it was often followed up by a cheery "hallo" on subsequent days.
- Listen to a new piece or type of music each day, a new musical instrument, a new radio station—the Internet offers almost infinite possibilities.

- Read a new type of book, article, journal, or magazine at the library.
- Walk or go by bus or train to a new place or by a new route or form of transport.

Politics, the media, and the Internet are easily available to older people. Possible projects are to identify particular groups of people—for example, particular disabilities, countries, regions, or local activities.

Projects are another important way of strengthening creativity in an older person's life. Some projects that I have seen are:

- Organizing and labeling family and personal photographs. This was taken on with writing a description of each event photographed, and then written portraits and biographies of everyone who appeared in the photos. People who become skilled in the use of computer programs that allow composite photos to be designed and printed may be able to make very interesting products.
- Creating a family tree. A lot of this used to involve visiting various record offices but may now be done on the Internet.
- Digitizing slides to electronic formats and making slide shows for a photo-viewer. Similarly, converting 8mm movies to DVD can bring family memories back to life.
- Organizing collections of music. Older people can be introduced to digital music players and creating their own playlists from favorite music.
- Organizing and labeling family letters and heirlooms.
- Taking photographs of every place that the older person had lived during a long life and labeling the collection.
- Writing a song about every member of the family or about friends. I suggest putting new words to existing music, but some musicians are able to compose or adapt their own music.
- Embroidery. Kits can be bought from craft stores, and the result can be framed and displayed.

Older people can also undertake creative projects. Here are some that I have come across:

- A photo-gallery of front-garden designs in the area on a photo-uploading Internet site

- Shop-window designs
- Dressing up in a lifetime collection of clothes, with a grandson taking photographs
- Interesting doors in the area—there are published posters of interesting doors and buildings of particular countries, why not something for every locality?
- Close-up photographs of all the flowers in the garden in a year, followed up next year by local parks managed by different park authorities
- A photo-gallery of badly kept areas of town uploaded to the Internet was brought to the attention of the local authority, local councilors, some large company headquarters, and the local press, which then went round to take their own photographs—it led to very rapid improvements

Many older people make important contributions to the family by grandparenting. While they are fit, child care or outings may be important and stimulating contributions to the family's human resources. To add creativity to activities such as this, people can be encouraged to ask wider questions about how it fits in their life. Grandparenting examples might include the following: How am I different from my grandparents? How are my children different from me as a parent?

Similarly, asking questions about the world around you is an important step in creativity. For example, older people might record information about the world as it was in photographs, uploading it to Web sites or making videos of interviews with people of their generation, and perhaps connecting it with public affairs and debates. For example, at the time of an important football game, people might ask: how is going to a game different or how are the lives of football players different from when I was young? A more intellectual project might be to compare Christianity with different religions or services in my church with the way they do it in other churches—people could visit different churches in the area and discuss how each was different. You can do this in theory or by asking other people in the care home. Some other ideas might be to approach thinking about an older person's current life situation. Examples might be the following: What do I think of having a longer life? How do I manage ill health so that I get some satisfaction in my life?

Thinking through Creativity in Older People's Lives:
A Dementia Garden

This section provides an example of thinking through creative possibilities.

PAUSE AND REFLECT: Gardens for People with Dementia

Many people, including older people, enjoy being outside and the activity of gardening. What might be the issues for an individual and organization in enabling people with dementia to use a garden? How could you resolve problems that might be raised?

Some Suggestions

For both individuals and organizations, the main concern is likely to be risk of wandering dangers within the garden. However, an area may often be secured and interesting but not dangerous with the right facilities provided. Having a garden available that is planned can be a safer way of achieving connection with past interests and the outside world than stopping people from using unsafe facilities. For example, having a water feature that allows hearing and touching moving water may be more suitable than a deep pond.

For someone with dementia, a suitable garden experience can bring a sense of connection with nature, make links with the past, and be stimulating and interesting if it offers variety, even if the person cannot express this directly. If the garden user is housebound, a garden can be made accessible to a wheelchair, a bed on wheels, or a chair that feels safe for the older person to be carried in. A garden can be made more interesting if it is stimulating to many different senses. Feeling secure in it will help, and usually a garden can also be made secure against someone with dementia wandering out. The following suggestions apply equally to changes that can be made in an older person's own garden and to the garden of a care home or day center. Some of the ideas can be adapted for use on apartment balconies.

- Walkways should have easy gradients so that someone with difficulty in walking can get around, or so a chair or bed can be wheeled to different positions.
- Walkways should also feature different surface textures, provided they are not too uneven for safety. Examples include: rough, smooth, different colors, gravel, tarmac with contrasting gravel inset, and different patterns of brick.
- Plantings should provide a variety of types and scents. Some plants such as lavender can be collected, dried, and used for craft activities and as a reminder of summer.
- Gardens should offer places to sit, convenient to have a drink brought to visitors, taking advantage of different areas of the garden and the views they provide, and places in and out of the sun at different times of the day. Also bear in mind protection from the wind.

- Different levels of planting should use different types and colors of container. Raised planting brings plants within reach to touch, smell, and view closely, and it enables some old people to work with plants themselves, dead-heading, planting, and cutting flowers for the house.
- Sculptures, gnomes, or other items for display, such as driftwood, pebbles, or stones, can provide different textures to stroke and touch.
- Plant specimens such as irises, lilies, or orchids, and striking bulbs or strangely shaped plants or bushes can stimulate interest and influence photography projects. Strong colors may benefit people with sight impairments.
- Climbing plants and bushes also vary the interest in a garden and provide opportunities for variation in lighting.
- Connected with this, screens and pergolas offer interesting dappled and shaded areas.
- Water can be interesting to sight, sound, and touch senses, especially moving water that makes a noise (although this may stimulate urination). Also of interest is water that can be touched or that contains fish (which may need to be protected from fishing birds).

LIFE REVIEW AND REMINISCENCE

Life review and reminiscence are important creative techniques that build on narrative approaches to practice, central to the citizenship view of practice set out in chapter 4. Reminiscence is mainly done in groups, and so is dealt with in the next chapter. These techniques are particularly powerful because they are natural acts that everyone does in their lives.

Life review comes from the idea that people live through a series of stages in life. Transition from one stage to the next can be facilitated by rational processing of experience of previous phases. This helps to bring out important issues in life, which may need resolving or correcting.

Life review is a one-on-one experience, performed between a client as the reviewer and a therapeutic listener (Burnside & Haight, 1992). The aim is to recall, examine, and evaluate the entire life span as a basis for making plans for the future. The process often examines the client's conscience and responsibility for what took place; it may therefore contain spiritual elements. It involves recalling both remote and recent events, and addressing both sad and happy times. Planning for the future, for example, death or an important decision, or dealing with a crisis may lead to identifying elements of the self—what has continued and what has changed—and evaluation of the events reviewed, what the client contributed and lost as a result of what happened.

Recent developments have included the use of narrative strategies to help people make connections between various events in their lives by telling a story. The practitioner may offer a questionnaire covering various phases or aspects of life a few days in advance of a meeting with the client. This helps clients to plan their narrative. Commonly, the questionnaire, in greater or lesser detail, covers:

- Childhood and family of origin
- Adulthood and work life
- The here and now—particularly focusing on the impact of the present phase of life, including aging, increasing disability, and approaching death, if this is relevant

Reminiscence work with individuals may help practitioners to understand aspects of clients' lives that are affecting them at present. It may also provide a basis for story writing, poetry, or music activities (Burnside & Haight, 1992). Life review is less concerned with producing a file of memories than with identifying and talking through issues or reevaluating issues in life.

Case Example: Mr. Hilton's Life Story

Mr. Hilton was an isolated older man living in social housing for many years. Increasingly disabled, he was considered at risk living on his own but resisted going into a care home or assisted living complex. The social worker sought to understand why this was. Rather than using a questionnaire, the practitioner went through the sequence of life phases listed above. She found he had had a happy childhood and had worked successfully in retail for many years, marrying and having two daughters. His wife had had an affair with a friend and left him, taking the two daughters. He had become depressed and drank too much, eventually losing his house. He had become a vagrant and lost his job. Eventually, he had been rescued by the Salvation Army, living first in an open hostel, then in a hotel-style facility before being rehoused. He had attempted to contact his daughters, now adults, but they had rejected him. He had gained a routine shop job and sought to maintain himself independently. Avoiding drinking meant that he rejected a social life and spent most of his time watching television or reading. Drawing out these various experiences, the social worker drew out his fear that a care home or assisted living would be a step back to the hostel experience, and he was unable to conceive of benefits he would get from any communal life or social contacts in care. She made suggestions about how the assisted living scheme in particular would help him pick up some of the enjoyable activities he had left behind him in his childhood and youth.

Life review in this way can be used to reevaluate shared experiences in people's lives. McDougall, Blixen, and Suen (1997) studied older homeless people with mental illnesses in six-week life review groups who were identifying shared themes in their reviews. These included anxiety about not being able to cope with future unexpected events; despair, feeling defeated and having no hope for things getting better; and helplessness, feeling unable to manage their affairs. As in this project, an important objective for practitioners undertaking life review work is to identify such feelings but also to find opportunities and possibilities in past experience or to identify a focus for interventions to reduce negative feelings. This can be achieved through solution-focused or cognitive behavioral practice or by providing social skills training to increase confidence in being able to tackle life problems.

CONCLUSION

The argument in this chapter is that if citizenship is to enhance the dignity of older people, there must be the opportunity of personal development, and creative practice together with the opportunity for creativity in an older person's life is an important aspect of achieving a good quality of life for older people. The sense of community in any care facility, for day attenders or residents, benefits from engagement in creative activity. I have also suggested that creativity can be achieved in many aspects of daily lives, even if those lives are circumscribed by disability and frailty.

FURTHER READING

The Creative Arts in Dementia Care: Practical Person-centered Approaches and Ideas, by J. Hayes (with S. Povey) (London: Jessica Kingsley, 2010).

The Creative Arts in Palliative Care, edited by N. Hartley and M. Payne (London: Jessica Kingsley, 2008).

These books provide useful discussion of issues in using creative arts with older people who suffer from dementia and in palliative care, respectively, and many practical ideas.

How to Make Your Care Home Fun: Simple Activities for People of All Abilities, by K. Agar (London: Jessica Kingsley, 2008).

A useful practical compendium of ideas and guidance.

Improving Learning in Later Life, by A. Withnail (Oxford: Routledge, 2010).

This research study reviews ideas about learning in later life and older people's experiences. It is a motivator to making efforts to stimulate learning opportunities for older people, while also recognizing the problems of doing so.

The Meaning of Reminiscence and Life Review, edited by J. Hendricks (Amityville, NY: Baywood, 2005).
A useful discussion and description of various uses of life review.

Internet Information

The U.S. National Center for Creative Aging has an extensive Web site with ideas for creativity and information resources: http://www.creativeaging.org.

Rosetta Life is an organization in the UK that promotes creative work among people who have cancer and/or are dying: there is a Web site, http://www .rosettalife.org, and YouTube video channel: http://www.youtube.com/user/ rosettalive.

Arts for Health Cornwall and Isles of Scilly describes an extensive project working with older people in care homes and in the community, including singing, dancing, painting, and other arts. The Web site includes staff and services users' quotations: http://www.artsforhealthcornwall.org.uk.

The resources page of Arts for Health, a long-established part of Manchester Metropolitan University in the UK, links to a wealth of reports and resources: http://www.artsforhealth.org/resources.

Access to Arts and Humanities Information and Resources
Worldwide arts resources: http://wwar.com.

The moving image gateway provides access to a wide variety of sound and video resources, many freely downloadable, that can be used for reminiscence or education activities: http://www.bufvc.ac.uk/gateway.

British History Online: http://www.british-history.ac.uk.

Canadian History on the Web: http://info.wlu.ca/~wwwhist/faculty/sneylan.

Polska (in Polish) site, http://www.polska.pl, and Poland (in English) site, http:// www.poland.pl/index.htm.

United States history: http://www.historesearch.com/ushist.html (includes videos).

All give access to a wide range of historical and modern resources. To find similar resources for other countries, an Internet search for "[country name] history resources" will usually produce helpful results.

On grandparenting, the Web sites of the UK Grandparents' Association, http:// www.grandparents-association.org.uk/index.php?option=com_content& view=frontpage&Itemid=1, and Grandparents.com, http://www.grandparents .com/gp/home/index.html, have many useful resources. The U.S. government

also offers a useful site for grandparents bringing up grandchildren: http://
www.usa.gov/Topics/Grandparents.shtml.

Thinking about Gardens

The Sensory Trust focuses on "creating inclusive environments": http://www
.sensorytrust.org.uk/welcome.htm.

Garden Visit.com provides an international listing of information about gardens
to give you useful ideas. You can search for sensory or sacred gardens or by
other types and get a worldwide list and information about them.: http://
www.gardenvisit.com.

The Association of Religious Communities assists the major religions to create
environments appropriate for expressing their beliefs. Gardens are an important part of this: http://www.arcworld.org/about_ARC.asp.

Group and Macro Practice with Older People

AIMS

This chapter explores how practitioners may develop groupwork and community work interventions to benefit older people in the community.

After working through this chapter, readers should be able to:

- Evaluate the main aims of groupwork interventions with older people
- Identify the main requirements of carrying out effective groupwork
- Explore reminiscence as an important use of groupwork with older people
- Evaluate the main aims of macro interventions with older people
- Understand useful macro interventions such as creating support groups and integrating older people into community groups
- Develop ways of enabling older people's participation in decisions that affect their lives and services for them

GROUPWORK AIMS

Why Groupwork with Older People?

Groupwork is an important offering in services for older people for many reasons:

- Humans naturally live much of their lives in groups, for example, families and social clubs, so interacting with groups is a necessary part of much social work practice.
- Older people sometimes become socially isolated and the opportunity of taking part in group activities is both a right as citizens and a benefit to psychological and emotional health.

- Care services are often provided in groups, in care homes or in day care, and in addition to working with people as individuals who just happen to be in a group, it enhances services to use the group as an element of practice.
- While groups may be used for psychotherapeutic treatment, a wide variety of other types of group occur in services, and practitioners who focus on the individual excluding the group may be missing the impact of group interactions on their clients.
- Groupwork can be particularly helpful in supporting informal caregivers.

Evans's (2009) research shows that an important way of developing quality of life in care homes is to create a sense of community among residents: groupwork may be an important way of doing so. On the other hand, people also have the right not to be in groups, and particularly in settings where groups are the norm, practitioners should provide for this.

Case Example: The Headteacher

A day center for older people that I was involved with provided a number of group activities alongside a medical check-up and lunch. One attender was a headteacher who said to me that he had been involved in group activities for many years in his work and preferred to sit in the garden or go for walks, whereas he valued the lunch and the check-up.

Finlay (1993) summarizes the special qualities that groups may bring to practice. For many people they may be good sources of:

- Sharing and support
- Energy and creativity
- Social learning
- Experience of heightened emotions
- Powerful norms and pressure for development or improvement
- Multiple relationships

This is so in part because groups used as part of services for older people recreate the emotions of earlier experience of groups in people's lives. The past experience may be positive or negative, so people may resist or embrace involvement in groups and may need to be helped to use them appropriately at this stage in their life.

Different types of group can be distinguished by looking at their main purposes:

- Exploring emotional or cognitive issues in people's lives—more psychotherapeutic in character
- Providing information, education, or practical experience
- Activity groups that help people have fulfilling and interesting experiences

Case Example: Groupwork in a Hospice

In the hospice where I work, there are activity groups formed around various creative activities and around physical exercise for people with disabilities. There are information or education groups for caregivers to receive teaching and share experiences about the financial problems of suffering from an advanced illness. More therapeutic groups for people who have learned that they are dying and for bereaved people or bereaved caregivers help members by enabling them to explore their personal reactions to their experience.

GROUPWORK PRACTICE

Planning

Doel (2006) usefully summarizes the main planning processes for a group. Practitioners should consider aims. These should include the help that you want to achieve and the main target membership. I would phrase the aims in the form of a statement about what the group members will be like at the end compared with the beginning: for example, "Better informed about ____," "More confident in ____," "More able to manage anger about ____." For the target membership, you might think about gender, age range, and different types of relationship.

Case Example: Family Members

I was involved in running a group for caregivers of older people. When we started to plan it, we had presumed that the attenders would be spouses, and had not expected referrals for brothers, sisters, sons, and daughters. This forced us to think about the focus on caregiving: Was it practical, so that anyone might share in the discussion? Or would discussion perhaps take an emotional turn? Spouses might have very different emotional needs from children and again from siblings. We decided to include siblings, but the emotions of children caring for older people might be very different and justified a separate group.

- Leadership. Who is going to be the main leader? There may also be other staff, including those who meet the group members as they arrive, see them out afterward (especially if it is in the evening, these may not be the same people), and those who prepare and serve refreshments.
- Group membership. What criteria are set for membership? Should it be open, so that new members might join after the beginning, or closed? Should there be a set number of sessions, or should the group continue? These questions are related: a continuing group will probably need to manage open membership, while a set membership probably means setting a time limit.
- Group sessions. How long and how frequent should sessions be? What time of day should they happen? Where should they be? Should there be a program? Are there any rules of behavior you want to set?

Case Example: Planning for Caregivers Groups

A social work team considered groups for spouse caregivers of older people with long-term physical disabilities. Discussing the options with a number of caregivers who, they thought, might attend, the team found that caregivers gave priority to practical tasks and being with their spouses. They did not want to use their scarce time away from caring tasks in unnecessary meetings. The team therefore carried out a survey to identify a program that caregivers thought would be useful and organized specific information-giving and education events, clear time limits to the number and length of sessions, and transport to and from the group. Mutual social support was programmed in before and after the information sessions. Later, the team provided groups for caregivers who had had very long experience of their caring roles. A similar survey found that these caregivers were more interested in the emotional consequences of their caring role and in sharing experiences and ways of coping as a form of mutual support. While they wanted fixed timings for sessions, they wanted an open-ended group, which met less frequently. They also preferred discussion topics, which they set at the previous session, rather than information.

As well as Doel's points, you may wish to consider:

- Ending. Particularly if you are planning a closed membership or time-limited group, how will you end it? Usually, you will want to think about how individuals leave, if they leave an open group, or how the whole group finishes. Will they meet up to evaluate the experience later? Will they be picked up afterward by the groupworkers or by other practitioners?

- Other colleagues. In many cases, your group will have members who are not your individual clients, so you have to plan feedback and any triggers, for example, for colleagues to follow up with people who do not attend.

- Practical arrangements. Some people will require transport to and from the group; you may also need to think about toilet and smoking arrangements.

- Equipment. If you are going to have activities, you may need flipchart paper and pens and other equipment for any activities you undertake.

Managing Groups

While a group may have general aims, it is usually also useful to help individual group members participate by clarifying in advance their aims or what they might hope to get out of participation. Policies about the way in which the group will be run and ground rules about maintaining confidentiality also need to be set at the outset. It works well if this is done by agreement, so that members feel greater commitment to these rules because they have participated in making them. Worries about what the group will be like, confusion or uncertainty about why people are attending, and lack of energy and commitment to attend can often be dealt with by careful explanation, reinforcement of those early discussions, agreeing to a formal contract for the group for a particular number of sessions, and by involvement in planning.

Among the difficulties in running a group are difficulties in relationships or conflicts between group members. Alternatively, individuals may be silent or fail to participate. Sometimes either leaders or group members may be anxious about expressing emotions or may fear that the group will heighten their emotions and they will become tearful or angry or unable to manage them. This can leave some people with a feeling of discomfort about their own or other people's emotions. Occasionally, it can cause people to leave the room. Conflicts, confrontations, and anger can be dealt with by having ground rules about behavior or establishing them at the point of a disagreement. Like emotions, it is often better to allow them to be expressed and encourage members of the group to listen to the issues raised by the emotions, making efforts to understand what is being expressed and talking about what they share. An appropriate approach to this is to generate an atmosphere of inquiry: Why is this important? How is it important in this life and in others' lives?

If one of the aims of the group is to enable people to express emotions or talk about experiences that have been difficult for them, it is useful to have more than one staff member. This allows different perspectives and responses to important feelings to emerge and also allows spare capacity if someone leaves the room; one of the staff members can go with them.

Case Example: Unexpected Revelations

I was a staff member in a group of middle-aged and older people discussing caring experiences. One woman group member talked at some length and with great feeling and anger about how she felt she had been forced by her husband to have sexual intercourse unwillingly in earlier stages of their marriage; she was now having to care for him. There was sympathy and support for her. Then two more revelations followed about unsatisfactory sexual experiences in marriage and a homosexual rape in childhood experienced by a male caregiver. Again the response was anger about some of the behavior experienced, empathy, sympathy, and support. The group facilitator eventually said that he was not certain that he should say this, but he felt it might help the group feel safer. So he stated that it was not a requirement of membership of the group to reveal past marriage or sexual experiences. Some time later, a further, less emotional experience was revealed: this disclosed sadness and hurt rather than anger and turmoil. Later again there was discussion about whether others had been stopped by the facilitator's intervention from discussing things that were important to them. There was also discussion about the fact that many different important issues had been covered in the group, how the group had been supportive, and that it felt okay. Feedback after the group was that it had been sometimes emotional but satisfactory to group members.

If, as a staff member, you are uncertain about intervening, it is a useful strategy to express that uncertainty when making the intervention and explain why you are doing so and comment on the reasons for your uncertainty. This allows the group to inquire into how the group is helpful or unhelpful and to consider the connections between shared experiences and the differences.

When an individual is leaving an open-ended group or a group is closing, it is helpful to allow time for leaving rituals, and to pick up experiences and feedback, either through a group evaluation some time after the event or through the practitioners working with group members individually. When someone fails to attend or leaves the group prematurely or unexpectedly, it is important to check what is happening and feed back to other group members any reasons for nonattendance or leaving.

Reminiscence Groups

Reminiscence is a well-established technique for working with older people usually undertaken as a group, mentioned in previous chapters. A systematic research review shows that it is more effective than medication in reducing depression in older people (Bohlmeijer, Smit, & Cuijpers, 2003); however, there is not good evidence that it is effective with the memory symptoms of dementia (Woods et al., 2005), although it may provide a useful social intervention. Sometimes there are structured questionnaires to elicit an organized response, but the research review does not show that this is more effective at lifting depression than unstructured discussion of reminiscences; this suggests that for social purposes a structured format is not likely to be required.

Reminiscence groups provide verbal interaction between people eliciting memories. Group leaders use visual, auditory, tactile, smell, and taste triggers to stimulate discussion (Hong, Heathcote, Quinn, & Plummer, 2005). Group members recall or tell each other about events or memorable early experiences. Recent events and experiences are excluded: this is not a therapeutic technique looking at the here and now. The aim is generally to increase interactions with peers, to focus conversations between them and to find commonalities. It can therefore be a technique that enhances a sense of equality between people. It may help to reduce isolation, increase self-esteem, and improve communication skills. It may also provide a basis for story writing, poetry, or music activities (Burnside & Haight, 1992).

Case Example: War Reminiscences among Older People

A group of older people in a London day care center agreed to spend two weeks talking about their war experiences. They brought official documents from this period—for example, ration books, magazines, and family photographs. Several had lost their homes in bombing and talked about being rehoused in unfamiliar parts of the city. Another rather younger person had been evacuated as a child to a rural area to avoid bombing. They discussed music from the period, and the following week some people brought music to perform and others brought old records to share. In another group of men, some had been in the armed forces and talked about experiences in traveling to distant parts of the world, and one had been in a prison camp. They compared this with well-known films about war.

Duffin's (1992) case studies of reminiscence groups in a hospital ward and a sheltered housing project emphasize:

- How recording, through written documents, audio, or video, gives importance to group members' words and values their input
- Ensuring staff approval and interest, and particularly making sure the senior staff are aware of how the groups will work and benefits they may have

- Finding an appropriate location separate from daily routines, to make the groups seem special, and to allow people to choose or refuse to attend

- Using exhibitions or reports to engage staff relatives who may be distant from the group's activities and give participants a sense of achievement and completion

- Identifying themes appropriate for and of interest to older people, such as childhood, home life, important shared experiences, and work life

Groupwork does not have to be in person: Kelly, Schofield, Booth, and Tolson (2006) taught older people in a rural area computer skills and then engaged them in a consultation on what older people wanted from community nursing services. This brings us to one of the important uses of groupwork: to stimulate participation in decision-making and community development.

MACRO INTERVENTIONS

Macro Practice: What and Why?

Macro social work interventions influence social structures and organizations to create the best environment and quality of life for older people. Macro practice is needed because, if older people are citizens, it is important that they can exercise their rights as citizens to plan and live their own lives and to participate in service development, planning, and strategic issues that affect the service they are receiving. In the other direction, state and professional services and family support cannot provide every service that older people need. Communities and societies need to find ways of organizing to contribute to the involvement, care, support, and personal development of older people—to understand what aging means to individuals and to society more generally. This is because:

- Aging and the needs of older people may be socially hidden. People in younger age groups do not always think or know about the social experience of older people. Lifestyles and cultural representations of the good life do not value aging and older people.

- Many older people feel socially isolated because busy younger people pursuing their lives are uninterested about them or impatient with them.

- People often do not think through their responsibilities for older people in their families, neighborhoods, and society in general.

- People have often not developed skills in communicating and interacting with older people.

In addition, we have seen that mainstreaming and age-proofing requires nonspecialist agencies—such as housing, police, emergency services, workplaces, and leisure facilities—to deal with older people. Social workers may be a resource to contribute knowledge, experience, and skill in relating to older people to the wider community.

The following sections build on previous sections on groupwork and look at building mutual support groups and organizations, integrating older people in wider community organizations, and helping older people to participate in service development.

Mutual Support Groups and Organizations

Organizing social support networks and groups has a long history in social work and is also well-established in health care. Increasingly, support groups are also available online through the Internet (Eysenbach, Powell, Englesakis, Rizo, & Stern, 2004). Support groups may be locality-based, in which case they often respond to the particular social needs of a housing facility or assisted living organization. Alternatively, they may form around particular medical conditions or disabilities, or particular social needs, such as bereavement. They may be for clients themselves, their supporters and informal caregivers, or other family members. Self-help groups are formed by the people affected themselves, sometimes with help or guidance from professionals. Support groups may also be created by professionals who identify a need within their agency or workload and as part of the agency's practice; these can sometimes be hard to distinguish from other kinds of groups. Groups may form around a particular need or locality or develop a long-term existence as a campaigning or support organization.

A basic requirement of mutual or other support groups is a shared personal identity that includes the issue that the group focuses on. Practitioners can form a link between professional help for these issues and people working together to deal with issues that face them, or to campaign for policy or social and cultural change. Although a campaigning role may be inappropriate to or resisted by an official social agency, it is a citizen's right to campaign and seek policy or social change on issues of interest to them. It must equally be a responsibility of a practitioner in that field to support that right. Moreover, the idea of expert patients and expert caregivers suggests that people who experience a disability or social situation every day gain expertise in managing it and in minor variations in that condition that can be very informative for practitioners.

While developing self-help and other support groups requires similar expertise to that of groupwork, practitioners need to be conscious of standing aside from influence. Members need to take responsibility for decisions and the overall direction of groups themselves. Practitioners are more appropriately advisers or consultants to groups. It is also useful to treat equally the leadership and the membership of groups where there is disagreement, since exclusive support for either may lead to conflict or difficulty in maintaining the group (Wilson, 1995).

Integrating Older People into Community Organizations

An important way in which practitioners can contribute to mainstreaming aging as an issue in society is by encouraging existing nonspecialist community organizations to support and include organizations for older people within their programs. This may offer additional activity or support groups. More important, it connects them with organizations in the community who can learn more about aging and engage with issues that aging presents in their communities. Practitioners might look for faith and church groups, work groups, and commercial organizations such as pubs and restaurants that could offer some opportunities for older people.

Case Example: A Meeting at a Dinner

A local dinner for organizations supporting volunteering included the regional manager of a chain of bars and pubs. He sat next to a volunteer organizer from a social work agency. One of the tasks of the organizer was to develop luncheon clubs for older people, but many older people found the volunteer catering at some of the church halls uninspiring. He asked whether some of the chain's pubs might have facilities to accommodate a luncheon club, providing a cut-price lunch because of the trade it brought in. The regional manager, it so happened, was worrying about the lunchtime trade in some of his suburban pubs. This marriage made in heaven ran into difficulties when some older people refused to take meals in bars, but the regional manager knew people who ran chains of cafes without a reputation for drinking alcohol, and the scheme extended. These arrangements were a useful supplement to the more conventional luncheon clubs.

This is, again, an example of mainstreaming practice.

PARTICIPATION BY OLDER PEOPLE IN
SERVICE PLANNING AND ORGANIZATION

A major reason for developing macro practice is to engage older people as citizens in influencing the management and policy that provides the strategic direction of their services. A variety of ways of involving older people in making decisions about the services they use has been reported (Janzon & Law, 2003). These include:

- User panels. These are useful where users meet in reminiscence groups, in a day center, or a care home. Attenders and residents can elect people to represent them in occasional discussions about issues of concern.

- Forums. This refers to one-off events about a topic of public concern—for example, a change in service or regular events that may have an information-giving focus.
- Elder councils. These might involve elections to a council for a period; it would meet regularly and discuss a range of topics.
- Qualitative in-depth interviews carried out by service managers in users' own homes. This would give more precise and complex information but loses the opportunity that groups and meetings offer for ideas from one user to spark creative responses from another.

Crawford, Rutter, and Thelwall (2003) identify a number of things that may get in the way of achieving effective participation by people in service delivery or development:

- Organizational barriers—for example, not having enough time or resources to bring about change
- Professional resistance and negative staff attitudes
- Concerns from staff and managers about how representative the service users are who participate and whether their views would be seen as valid by the whole range of service users
- Difficulty in managing the expectations and demands of service users—for example, users may want changes that go against political or organizational priorities, and it is difficult for services to respond to their wishes

Most participation projects fall down because service users do not see real and immediate change from their suggestions; they then become disillusioned. RIPFA (2007) identifies four factors that research evidence suggests will help in achieving good results from participation projects with older people:

- Participation projects should be managed by organizations providing services to older people and should specify the questions that they want answered so that discussion is well-focused and relevant to something that the provider is actually able and wants to carry out. Being too directive may make service users feel disempowered, so it is important to balance focus with flexibility. Approaches reported included: reading groups looking at information, guidance documents and books about the topic; surveys carried out by groups of

Social Exclusion Issues

AIMS

This chapter focuses on three aspects of practice with older people concerned with social exclusion:

- Where aging interacts with inequalities in people's lives
- Safeguarding older people so that they achieve both psychological and social security
- Responding to end-of-life issues, loss, and bereavement in old age

AGEISM AND SOCIAL INEQUALITIES

Two issues about inequalities are likely to affect practitioners with older people: ageism and the impact on older people of wider health inequalities. These are both situations in which the social order—recurring patterns of social relations in society—leads to older people being discriminated against or excluded from their citizenship or ordinary human relationships and social networks.

Ageism

The Anti-Ageism Taskforce of the (U.S.) International Longevity Center (2006, p. 21) identifies four different aspects of ageism that relate to older people: (1) individuals' ideas, attitudes, beliefs, and practices; and (2) organizations' missions, rules, and practices that are (3) biased against persons or groups based on their older age, (4) whether unintentionally (carried out without the perpetrator's awareness that they are biased) or intentionally (carried out with the knowledge that they are biased, including carrying out practices that take advantage of the vulnerabilities of older people).

Ageism affects people throughout their lives. Younger people may suffer ageism because they are feared as violent, uncontrolled, noisy, immature, and incompetent through lack of experience. People in midlife may be affected by many prejudices about their age. A UK employers' association gave people at all levels in commercial and industrial organizations a series of scenarios at a time when antidiscrimination legislation was being extended to aging. The aim was to evaluate their attitudes about acceptable behavior toward older people. The main findings are set out in box 8.1. Although many people were aware of age discrimination as an issue, they were unclear about appropriate actions as managers and employees.

PAUSE AND REFLECT: Examples of Ageism

The Anti-Ageism Task Force (2006) identifies a range of aspects of ageism: elder abuse and discrimination in health care, nursing homes, emergency services, the workplace, the media, and in marketing. Think about each of these areas and identify examples of ageism that you have experienced, observed, or read about in the press.

Box 8.1 Ageist Attitudes in Working Life (Employers' Forum on Ageing, 2006)

Scenarios	Main findings
Paying an older person more than a younger person, regardless of experience.	A third of people think that it is not discriminatory to pay someone based on their age.
Managing people differently depending on their age (targets enforced less or more aggressively).	36% think that people should be managed differently because of their age.
Not employing or keeping someone on because their appearance doesn't match the company's image.	39% believe that if someone's perceived age doesn't match the company's image they should not be employed.
Assuming the oldest person you meet in a meeting is the most "senior."	39% think that it is reasonable to assume that the oldest person in the room is the most senior.
Employing someone of a similar age to you and your colleagues, to ensure a good team "fit."	40% think that employing people of similar ages to ensure "team fit" is fair.
Not giving someone a job because they have too little/too much experience.	62% are aware of age discrimination legislation.

Some Suggestions

Some of the things I thought about were: a man who refused to provide informal personal care for his chronically sick long-term partner because she "no longer interested" him; press reports of doctors giving priority to transplants for younger rather than older patients; care homes limiting the proportion of residents with dementia to preserve an active social group; short-staffed ambulance services taking young people to hospital with acute illnesses rather than taking older people on regular transport to day care; difficulty for middle-aged people in getting jobs; younger presenters (particularly women) being preferred to older presenters on television; and marketing that presents cosmetics as antiaging.

The ease with which examples come to mind suggests that societies have focused too readily on the value of younger people and a higher valuation of the image of youth. Cultural stereotypes construct older bodies and looks as repulsive. In avoiding ageism, practitioners will need to focus on two issues:

- Preventing ageism affecting their own or their team's practice
- Intervening to prevent ageism affecting services with which they come in contact

Case Examples: Identifying and Responding to Ageism

The social worker working with a surgical team accompanied the medical and nursing team on a ward round, in which the progress of each patient was discussed in turn by the patient's bedside. One patient was a man in his seventies affected by heart disease, but with a large number of other problems, which meant that he needed a nursing home place. A successful operation had been carried out, but he had remained in the hospital for several weeks awaiting a place. The lead doctor called him a "bed-blocker" and insisted to the social worker that he should be discharged to any care home, even if it was not close to his home and friends. Later, a man in his eighties with chronic lung disease was making very slow progress, and his similarly aged wife was, reported the social worker, extremely anxious about managing his disability at home. However, because there was care at home, the lead doctor determined that he should be discharged home immediately, releasing a bed for another patient awaiting an operation. Later again, a man in his fifties who had experienced a serious coronary thrombosis and had recovered well had a wife who was away on business, leaving a son (nineteen) and daughter (sixteen) at home, and was not discharged for a further week until she returned home and was able to care for him.

Part of the social worker's approach to these situations was, working in association with nurses, to manage the discharge arrangements so that the lead doctor's decisions were implemented in ways that were more advantageous to patients and families than the original decision. Secondly, she regularly reported back to doctors and nurses about the processes of discharge, so that they were regularly updated and informed about the interpersonal consequences of decisions. Third, rather than confronting the ageism implicit in this run of decisions in a meeting with all staff, she took an informal opportunity to talk it through with the doctor. This got her labeled "Miss Equality," but in the good-humored exchange, the doctor acknowledged the inconsistencies. Pushed into a corner in public with other staff present, he might have been more defensive and insistent on his position. This sort of situation continued to arise but slowly declined, with the occasional "Miss Equality" comment as a joking reference to the issue. These exchanges made it clear that the lead doctor was well aware of the nurse and social worker management of the progress of these cases; the situation moved toward a mutual recognition that the whole team had a duty to maintain progression of patients through the system, while not inappropriately disadvantaging or discriminating against them.

Inequalities

Citizenship social work is concerned about older people's rights to equality and fairness in service provision. Since only a quarter of differences between people are genetically determined (Just Ageing, 2009a) there is much scope for intervention in early and mid-years to reduce ill health and poverty in later years. Practitioners need to understand inequalities affecting older people both to contribute to reducing such inequalities in macro interventions and in their professional work and also to avoid acting unfairly in their work.

Three different types of inequality are relevant:

- Inequality between different groups within the same generation of older people or age cohort
- Inequality between different generations of people living at the same time or intergenerational inequality
- Unequal experiences over the life course, at different life stages, for each individual (Just Ageing, 2009a)

Three major causes of inequality in health, housing, and social care are:

- Differences because some people did not recognize or accept that they needed services
- Differences because some people were not aware that services were available
- Differences in people's ability to make themselves heard and to navigate service systems (Just Ageing, 2009b)

What relevant factors does research identify? First, people with better education have a lower risk of poverty and of ill health. Stable employment and marriage also strengthens economic security and good health as people age (Just Ageing, 2009a, pp. 10–14). People need to realize that they will probably live longer than they think and plan for this.

Wide-scale population-level interventions may lead to problems. For example, helping people to stay in work after official retirement age may disadvantage the health of people from lower socioeconomic groups, who are more likely to have physically demanding manual work than middle-class people. Policy and practice also needs to avoid making intergenerational conflict worse, for example, supporting free transport for older people, while still requiring children and poor students to pay for public transport. Obviously, all intervention advantages one group over another. Practitioners therefore need to look carefully at decisions they make to identify unfairnesses with other people in the same age cohort or in other cohorts.

Some groups of older people may suffer particularly from discrimination and prejudice. People from minority ethnic groups in the UK, for example, have poorer and less secure housing, are poorer in their ownership of consumer durables, have lower income, are less likely to have an additional pension from employment, and more likely to rely on state income support. On the other hand, there is considerable variation between minority ethnic groups, where Indian groups have similar levels of multiple deprivation to the majority white population; but higher proportions of people from Pakistani, Bangladeshi, Black Caribbean, and white Irish population groups are likely to have medium or higher deprivation (Evandrou, 2000). A similar pattern in the U.S. suggests that it is poverty affecting early life chances that accumulates health inequalities and disability throughout life. Poor older people are thus more likely to have disabilities and chronic ill health. They are further disadvantaged by not having had the chances to develop healthy behaviors and learn the skills of accessing appropriate health care (Reyes-Ortiz, 1999). Patel (2003) surveys policy and services for older people in minority ethnic communities in several European countries. While policy initiatives have tried to develop appropriate services for older people in minority ethnic groups, further work is required to do this well.

Box 8.2 sets out in diagrammatic form the social determinants of the health argument. While we can see health inequalities in any society, we tend to focus on health behaviors, such as smoking and poor nutrition, that are the immediate cause of inequality. However, these behaviors are determined by the consequences of poverty and other factors. There is little point in tackling the behaviors without removing their source in the social determinants. The World

Box 8.2 The Social Determinants of Health

Health inequalities

Health behaviors, e.g., smoking

Consequences of social determinants,
e.g., poor education

Social determinants of health, e.g., poverty

Health Organization (WHO) established a Commission on the Social Determinants of Health (2008) and developed a program based on its three major recommendations:

- Improving daily living conditions for people across the world
- Tackle the inequitable distribution of power, money, and resources, which feeds into health inequalities
- Measure and understand the problem and assess the impact of action

These aims are important because, if we look at present health outcomes internationally, inequalities are widespread, and these inequalities arise from the impact of wider social inequalities, in particular poverty and its consequences. Therefore, efforts at improved professional care, while valuable, do not tackle the origins of these inequalities. Nevertheless, professional experience about the consequences of health inequalities for clients enables practitioners to hear from clients' narratives the history of how these sources of inequality have affected them.

Some minority groups are affected by the consequences of social stigma as well as by the poverty–education–ill health nexus in creating inequalities in old age. For example, because lesbian/gay/bisexual/transgender (LGBT) people may interact with officialdom for the first time in their lives as they need health and social care services, the domestic arrangements that reflect their sexuality may be disclosed to friends and family for the first time as they need services in old age (Addis et al., 2009). The following case examples describe situations I have come across.

Case Examples: Jane and Elizabeth; Conrad

An older woman, Jane, was admitted to a care home from her apartment, which she shared with a longstanding friend, Elizabeth, whom Jane's brothers and sister disliked. They asked the friend to make other living arrangements and leave the apartment so that it could be sold. On a visit to the care home, one of Jane's brothers was shocked and angry when he found Jane and Elizabeth in bed together. There was a furious argument, and care workers had to mediate by separating the brother and Elizabeth in different rooms. A social worker was asked to sort out the problems. She saw different members of the family separately. It seems the sister and one brother had assumed that Jane and Elizabeth had a lesbian partnership (though this had never been discussed), while the brother who caused the fuss had assumed it was a flat-sharing arrangement. A lesbian relationship was unacceptable to his Christian worldview. The social worker spent some time talking through his anger and distress, which increased when it was revealed that Jane had left all her property to Elizabeth in her will and asked that Elizabeth arrange her funeral. This public acknowledgment of their relationship was unacceptable to all of Jane's brothers and sisters. The care home workers arranged different visiting times for Elizabeth and Jane's family, to separate them as far as possible. When Jane died, the social worker worked out an arrangement with Elizabeth to ask an acceptable minister of religion to organize a special memorial event for members of Jane's family; some also went to the funeral, but some did not. This case example describes a common situation in which care arrangements make transparent issues of sexuality that had been hidden or dormant. The practitioner's approach here was to maintain participation of the people who are important to the client: sometimes this requires facing up to sexual difference; sometimes separate arrangements help everyone to participate.

Conrad, an older man, affected by renal disease, had regular dialysis, which was eventually arranged at home, where he lived in a longstanding marriage with his wife, often visited by his adult children. However, he became very distressed at a hospital appointment and was referred to the renal social worker. She discovered that, unknown to his wife, he had a long-standing homosexual relationship with a man and felt that he wanted his male partner to be with him during his treatments since he was no longer able to see him regularly. The social worker talked through various options with Conrad, including complete openness, and a range of other possibilities. He decided not to disclose his bisexuality, and the social worker arranged transport to include time for his male partner in his visits to the hospital for assessment by renal physicians. The social worker also talked through with him how they would handle his death and funeral in ways that would involve his male partner. They decided on separate good-byes and a shared ritual before the death that the partner could use for memorialization of their relationship. This is an example of a practitioner raising end-of-life issues as a normal part of work with older people.

SAFEGUARDING OLDER PEOPLE

Working with older people obviously involves safeguarding their rights and interests in many different ways; failure to permit them the full exercise of their human rights excludes older people from full citizenship. Citizenship social work focuses on what will help people to be secure. Security may be both physical and emotional and has a number of different aspects in practice:

- Physical security—for example, avoiding unwanted change, accidents, violence, or fear of them
- Legal security—for example, feeling that the law and administrative procedures protect them
- Self-security—being respected and valued by others (Payne, 2011, ch. 8)

In social care, security can be enhanced by support and caring practice that include:

- Dialogue and narrative that enables people to know that practitioners have built up an understanding of the situation as clients see it
- The security of knowing that regular checks will be made efficiently, for example, by maintaining regular telephone contacts.
- Demonstration of forethought and planning using advance care planning

The range of possible issues that arise in safeguarding are suggested by legal responsibilities. For example, in an authoritative UK legal text, Mandelstam (2009) covers the following issues:

- The policy and legal responsibilities of health, social care, and emergency services for responding to the needs of vulnerable adults

- The regulation of care provision
- Arrangements for dealing with mental incapacity that may mean that adults cannot make their own decisions about their lives
- Arrangements for protecting the safety of the environment of older people, for example, housing and local community safety
- Protecting older people from physical and sexual harm and abuse
- Protecting older people from financial abuse, not only by family members but by commercial and financial service providers

The following two sections examine two areas where social care practitioners are likely to be involved: where protection in an emergency may be needed; and in matters of physical, sexual, emotional, and financial abuse.

Safeguarding: Disasters and Crises in the Community

Just like anyone else, older people may be involved in a crisis or disaster in their community, but to regain security, services need to consider their particular needs. Social workers involved in responding to crisis events can often provide leadership and expertise to make sure that older people are resecured. Such disasters may include natural disasters like landslides, earthquakes, and floods, and human-caused disasters, such as major road accidents, aircraft crashes, chemical explosions, or terrorism.

Such disasters go through phases. There may be a feeling of threat or anxiety. Then comes the impact of the actual accident or event. First there is a rescue or heroic phase of reaction. After this, there is a honeymoon phase, where people feel they have coped well with the immediate problems. In the longer term, there may be an inventory phase, in which people check their thoughts and feelings with others and work out what they have lost, individually and collectively. A disillusionment phase may follow in which people feel that they have not fared well in recovering from the event: perhaps they have increased physical or emotional difficulties. Finally there is a phase of reconstruction or recovery (Oriol, 2005). As with all stage analyses of human reactions to events, people will not necessarily go through each phase, or in the set order. This analysis, however, helps to identify issues that older people may experience.

Everyone is affected individually. They may feel that the disaster is such a blow to their normal defenses and way of life that they cannot manage their life effectively. Collective effects may arise when social supports and relationships are adversely affected. Older people may be particularly affected because:

- Their diminished senses of sight, smell, and hearing may mean that they miss warning signs.

- They may respond slowly to events.
- Chronic illness and special dietary needs may place them at greater risk than younger people.
- Losses may be compounded. If they are already bereaved or isolated, further losses may occur because of a disaster.
- They may reject help or not be able to cope with the bureaucracy associated with official responses to a disaster.
- They are more vulnerable than younger people to hypo- or hyper-thermia (loss of body heat or overheating).
- They may be distressed because they have to move, for example, from their own home or from a care home.
- They may have poor reading or language skills because of cultural differences or sensory disabilities.

We can help with these problems by:

- Providing strong and continual verbal reassurance (provided this is realistic)
- Helping to recover physical possessions, checking on the home regularly, and arranging for someone to be with them
- Giving special attention to making sure they are rehoused, if possible in familiar surroundings and with people that they know
- Helping to reconnect people with family or social contacts
- Getting medical or financial help
- Checking what medication they require and reestablishing the correct treatment regimes
- Escorting them so that they feel safe when they need to move around (Oriol, 2005)

Most social workers do not work in disaster relief services, but these ideas are relevant to a lot of situations that they might be called upon to deal with.

Case Example: Elise's Flood

Elise, in her late seventies, had been housebound and receiving social services for a number of years in a small house that was below street level. In an exceptionally long rainy period, the drains in the street were blocked, and a heavy torrent led to the ground floor of her house being flooded by more than three feet of water. She telephoned her son, who contacted the emergency services. They pumped out the water and installed an industrial dryer to dry out the house. Her son also called the social care agency, and Elise's regular care worker dropped her usual round and called on Elise. She called the social worker who was Elise's case manager, who also visited at once. She transported Elise to a local church hall, which was providing an emergency center for people affected by the flood. The care worker helped Elise to pack some clothes, medication, and valuable property and went with her to the hall. There Elise could get hot food, watch television, and also talk to other people. Although it was drying out, the house was very dirty and smelly and could not be reoccupied immediately. Discussing this with Elise, who was finding the families with children at the hall noisy and disturbing, the social worker arranged for her to stay at a local care home. Over the next six weeks, she and the care worker visited Elise regularly, took her home to look at the progress of repairs and redecoration, and to collect more personal items to take back to the care home. The son did the redecorating, although a voluntary group of church members helped people who did not have relatives. All of these actions reflect a careful response to this disaster in Elise's life, which made sure she felt secure and was able to reestablish a secure lifestyle again.

Safeguarding: Abuse and Neglect of Older People

Concern about the possibility that older people are being abused or neglected by family members or caregivers has been rising in many Western nations since the 1980s. Two areas initiated concern. One is abuse in care homes, including nursing homes. The other area is an extension of domestic violence, where physical or other abuse is by caregivers. A widely quoted definition of abuse focuses on the human rights of older people: "a violation of an individual's human and civil rights by another person or persons" (Home Office/Department of Health, 2000).

Among the types of abuse that older people may experience are:

- Physical abuse—including hitting, slapping, over- or misuse of medication, undue restraint, or inappropriate sanctions
- Sexual abuse—including rape and sexual assault, or sexual acts to which the vulnerable adult has not or could not consent and/or was pressured into consenting
- Psychological abuse—including threats of harm or abandonment, humiliation, verbal or racial abuse, isolation, or withdrawal from services or supportive networks
- Financial or material abuse—including theft; fraud; pressure around wills, property, or inheritance; and misuse or misappropriation of benefits

- Neglect—including failure to access medical care or services, negligence in the face of risk-taking, failure to give prescribed medication, poor nutrition, or lack of heating (Welsh Assembly, 2000)

Self-neglect is an important category of behavior, which is widespread across the world (Fallon, 2006). Intervening is difficult because older people's autonomy prevents professionals from being engaged, and self-neglect may also isolate the older person so that the problems are not reported or are reported inappropriately, as presenting housing problems or public health hazards. The social work approach to such issues is to try to build a relationship with the older person, identify what is important and not important to them, and try to carry out improvements with them. If practitioners engage cleaning services, it is helpful to be with the older person as cleaners do their work. Cognitive behavioral therapy to try to reduce the impact of fears may also be helpful, if the older person has some insight into the deterioration of his or her environment and wants change.

A systematic study of prevalence studies across the world (Cooper, Selwood, & Livington, 2008) found that 6 percent of the older population, 25 percent of vulnerable adults, and a third of family caregivers report being involved in significant abuse, but only 1 to 2 percent of this is reported officially. However, if they are directly asked, older people and their caregivers are prepared to report it, so it is important to ask. People may report abuse when they want services to do something about it, although they may also try to avoid having caring relationships disrupted. Cultural attitudes may be important in reporting. In a study comparing Polish and U.S. women's and men's attitudes to "intimate violence," the U.S. discourse was about men gaining power over women, while the Polish discourse was about how violence was a negative factor in relationships (Klein & Kwiatkowska, 1999).

Fallon (2006) reviews a variety of suggestions for identifying typical kinds of victims and perpetrators; I have adapted some of the terminology in the following summary and would be cautious about trying to classify people too closely. Intervention needs to deal with the individuality of abusive or neglectful situations. Frail, isolated older people, especially very old people, are most likely to be abused. Victims of psychological and physical abuse may be in good health but live with a perpetrator on whom they are financially dependent. Victims of neglect tend to be very old with physical and mental incapacity that is stressful for their informal caregivers. Victims of financial abuse are financially independent and therefore live alone, being socially isolated and sometimes rather eccentric in behavior. It may be helpful to identify different types of perpetrators.

Overwhelmed perpetrators are often competent caregivers who are unable to cope with increasing care needs, while impaired perpetrators may not have appropriate caring skills for very dependent older people. Exploiting perpetrators get involved with older people for their own benefit, which may be financial or self-satisfaction as a contributor to family or community. Bullying perpetrators manage their behavior to appear reasonable, while enjoying controlling others, or move toward sadistic behavior, enjoying humiliating or frightening people.

Practitioners should also look out for situations in which people are likely to be highly stressed as caregivers. A cross-European study (including Poland) of family care suggests that some social factors that lead to people experiencing their care for family members as a burden are similar to risk factors in elder abuse. "Several studies suggest that the risk for both increases in case of cohabitation, of high amounts of care provided, when the care recipient presents behavioral disturbances, when the carer suffers from depression and low self-esteem, when a negative relationship between carer and elder existed already in the past, and when the carer does not feel supported by formal services" (Lamura et al., 2008).

Case Example: A Mentally Ill Older Woman and Her Son

An elderly woman with a history of mental illness was becoming increasingly frail. She managed well at home, although her behavior was often bizarre and sometimes violent. Her adult son lived with her. He worked on building contracts and was usually in regular employment. However, advised by her doctor that his mother was becoming increasingly frail, he took a period away from working to look after her. She later complained to her mental health social worker that he had hit her on a number of occasions. The social worker interviewed the son privately about these allegations, which he admitted were true. He felt ambivalent, valuing himself because he was making an effort to care for his mother. However, he had also been feeling isolated and that he was wasting his life caring for a very difficult older woman. The social worker discussed with him a number of ways in which he could manage his anger and frustration. It was important to recognize both the contribution he was making as well as the difficulties in the relationship. The mother was happy to have his care, although she could not always control the symptoms of her illness.

This case, as well as illustrating the mixed feelings that are common in such situations, also shows that various protective devices can often be achieved. Practitioners can often organize an increase in regularity of visiting to check on clients' circumstances by coordinating visits made by different professionals.

Fallon (2006) describes New Zealand provision for older citizens, identifying four elements of a safeguarding service:

- Local services to support older people and respond to difficult or risky situations
- Professional health and social care interventions to help and protect individuals experiencing abuse and neglect
- Advisory group support for professionals engaged in this difficult work and local coordinators of services
- National policy development and coordination

The starting point of investigations of allegations of abuse is to contact all the professionals involved and informal and community caregivers, if possible, to see the extent to which concerns are shared. Many professionals may have picked up signs of abuse, and when these are coordinated by a case conference or similar meeting, a pattern of problems may emerge. Strategies for protection may then be worked out between agencies. The autonomy of adults means that in many legal systems no direct intervention can be made, for example, to remove an abuser or shift a victim to a safe place. However, much abuse is a criminal offense, and legal action may be possible, which may be a warning to perpetrators of abuse and protect the client. Some jurisdictions make legal interventions possible. For example, in Scotland, the Adult Support and Protection (Scotland) Act 2007 requires local social services authorities to promote cooperation between agencies and to make inquiries if allegations come to their attention. It also provides for legal orders to require assessments to the situations that are identified to be carried out, to remove someone who is at risk from a particular situation, or to ban an abuser from being present in the home of an abused person.

END-OF-LIFE AND BEREAVEMENT ISSUES

End-of-Life Services

For older people, physical frailty and receiving help from age-related services may remind them that moving into older age also means moving toward the end of life. Therefore, practitioners with older people need to be aware of end-of-life issues and be ready to raise and deal with them. To fail to do so may exclude older people from resolving interpersonal relationships before their death, leave the family with unresolved relationship problems, and exclude people from the right to die well.

End-of-life care services are of three kinds:

- Palliative care is a multiprofessional practice in which pain and symptom control is combined with concern for the psychological, social, and spiritual issues that arise for someone who is dying and the family and community around them. It developed from services for people with cancer and other serious diagnosed illnesses, and is a fairly short-term service with important medical and nursing input.

- End-of-life care is the provision of care services for people who are approaching the end of life. It has developed more recently, from a recognition that most people come to a phase of life in which they become increasingly frail, with perhaps several illnesses affecting them at the same time. In this situation, people may not need or receive extensive specialist medical and nursing help, but their families and people around them and non-specialized health and social services in their community need to focus not only on the daily pressures of dealing with increasing frailty, but also the reality that this signals the approach of the end of life. This is sometimes known as nonspecialist or general palliative care.

- Supportive care is care for people receiving continuing and often long-term treatment for an advanced and potentially life-threatening disease, which has not yet reached its end-stage. They are in "survivorship," managing a life that includes living with an illness that may eventually lead to their death. Some people in survivorship will die from some cause other than the major disease that they have survived, but they are all people who are aware that they have survived a major medical crisis in their lives (Reith & Payne, 2009).

Each of these different situations gives rise to different psychological and social reactions, from patients and from the people in their families and communities. An important issue is awareness: how far do people experiencing physical symptoms and their families know that this will soon lead to death (Glaser & Strauss, 1965, 1968)? Whatever their level of awareness, many people at the end of life attach great importance to hope and ways of sustaining it, which may include their spiritual or religious beliefs. Pattison (1977) suggests that for many people there are several phases:

- A period when people know they have an illness that might be fatal: "the potential death" phase

- An event when they are told or come to know that they are expected to die: "the crisis knowledge of death"—people have vivid memories of being told that they are expected to die, so how this is done is very important for their adjustment within the dying process
- A subsequent period of anxiety as they come to accept the prognosis: "the acute crisis phase" reaches a peak
- A subsequent period of declining anxiety during which they live with the knowledge of their impending death: "the chronic living-dying phase"
- The terminal phase, where physical and social factors are increasingly disabling people from achieving desired objectives within a good quality of life, leading to—
- The point of death

Helping People Die Well

One of the aims of end-of-life, palliative, and supportive care is that people should be helped to die well; older literature refers to a "good death." Dying well might be interpreted variously by different individuals and ethnic and faith groups, so research into people's views has tried to make clearer what we are trying to achieve. Dying well includes both medical and social ideas such as:

- Removing the impact of physical symptoms, such as pain
- Reducing psychological and social stress both for the dying person and for their family and social network
- More controversially, making available the freedom to end life at the choice of the dying person if they cannot or do not want to continue to suffer unmanageable physical, psychological, and social stresses associated with the dying process
- Byock's (1997) discussion of dying well focuses on seeing this positively in having peace and being able to take up the possibilities offered by moving toward the end of life

Kellehear's (1990) important Australian study of one hundred people dying of cancer identified five aspects of dying well:

- Awareness of dying, usually derived from others' advice, particularly medical diagnosis and prognosis

- Social adjustments and personal preparation
- Public preparation, including legal, financial, religious, funeral, and medical arrangements
- Disengagement from work, which may be gradual or partial for some time
- Farewells

Interventions with Dying People and Their Families

Social work practice at the end of life involves, first, engaging with people at a time that they are aware that they are facing end-of-life issues. This can seem an intensely private area of people's lives, and practitioners may be concerned about raising an issue when the client does not want to discuss it or, on the other hand, provoking great emotion and distress, which they do not feel ready to handle.

On the first point, it is important to build awareness of statements about current problems or future progress, which may hint at a wish to talk about the end of life. Clients may say, for example, "I really feel I'm going downhill at the moment," or, "I'm feeling much worse now than I was a year ago." One reason for responding to such statements is to identify changes that should be reported to a doctor or nurse for investigation. Practitioners might respond by saying, "What is it about your life (or "your symptoms") that makes it worse at the moment?" The other reason is to broach concerns about end-of-life issues appropriately. For example, practitioners might respond with comments such as, "Are you perhaps worrying that you're never going to get back to the kind of lifestyle you want?" There is no need to worry that such questions will lead to unmanageable reactions, since it is easy for clients to close off the conversation if they do not want to take up the option of discussing the progression of their condition or situation.

On the second point, many older people have thought through end-of-life issues for themselves and are happy to discuss, for example, changes in living arrangements or plans for their funeral. If a lot of emotion or distress emerges, the most important reaction is to listen carefully to the issues that provoke the most feeling, since these can be taken up for resolution in practical ways over a period. It may also be necessary for the practitioner to apologize for "setting off something that is so distressing," while making the point that this may still be important for the client to think through. Many people wait for the professional to raise important issues and will not respond until the practitioner makes it clear that it is appropriate, no matter how important it is to them. Even though emotions are difficult at the time, they often appreciate the opportunity for discussion and value the practitioner for raising difficult issues.

Merely listening, however, is not enough. The most important reasons for facilitating these important discussions about end-of-life issues are:

- To generate a sense of openness in the professional relationships, so that it may be extended to other relationships in the client's life
- To permit advance care planning, so that the client's preferences for care arrangements can be established while they are still able to express them

Openness is important because it allows that an appropriate balance between hope for a further period of good quality of life can be balanced against a realistic assessment of the current progress of a client's frailties or medical conditions. A useful way of entering such discussion can be to ask clients to compare what they can do now with what they could do three months or some other period previously. As we saw in the more general context of practice in chapters 4 through 6, it is important to ask specifically about capabilities and to ask for clear comparisons, rather than asking conventionally, "How are you today?" which usually produces a standard polite response like, "I'm fine, thank you," or, "My old bones are creaking a bit today."

Openness about dying is also important because it allows family members to plan for the process of dying. For example, some people think it best to "protect" children or family members with learning difficulties from knowing what is going on as a relative is dying. However, most children and disabled people pick up the emotional responses of others in the family and the practical changes that take place, and may blame themselves for something going wrong or feel excluded if they are not kept informed. They will eventually have to deal with the death when it occurs, and being involved in the process of dying usually helps them to do so; distress is appropriate.

Case Example: Sam Dying at Home

Sally arranged for Sam, her dying father, to stay in her home, but told her children aged eight and ten years that he was staying while he was recovering from hospital treatment. However, the children seemed to be becoming edgy, and their behavior was difficult. Sam's social worker spoke with Sally about talking with them, and when she did so, she found that they had been worried by the physical changes in Sam's body and thought that he may not be improving because they had been noisy around the house. She explained that Sam had been receiving treatment, but was not expected to recover from his illness, so she was doing her best to care for him until he died. She engaged them in playing cards with Sam for half an hour every evening. At various times over the next few weeks, the children asked questions about death and dying and the funeral as these became important to them. Their behavior problems disappeared, since they were now able to participate in Sally's caring and in family life once again.

In addition to providing appropriate services for older people who are approaching the end of life, it is important also to help people complete life tasks that may be important to them. This may include life reviews and memorializations, such as memory boxes about the life events shared with children or grandchildren, information that identifies the older person's contribution to family and community history. This may be an important source of identity for the older person and also for other people as part of the family. Other life tasks may include getting in touch with friends and family members to say:

- Good-bye
- Thank you—for the importance of their relationship with the older person and for help and support provided as frailty or illness has increased
- Sorry—for any conflict or difficulty between them in the past
- I love you—an expression of the bonds between them

Practitioners may also need to help older people or their families cope with emotional reactions to dying. These may include:

- Shock and denial—"This can't be happening to me"
- Anger, rage, resentment, bitterness—"It's not fair, I've always tried to live a healthy lifestyle, and now I have this illness"
- Bargaining—"If I improve my nutrition or get fitter, I am going to overcome this illness"
- Depression—"I just can't be bothered keeping the house clean; I'll be dead soon and it'll be someone else's responsibility"

As originally formulated by Kübler-Ross (1969), through her research interviews with dying people, these were seen as stages in reaction to loss. However, while they are common emotions in people who are dying, they do not occur in any particular order, and not everyone experiences all of them. It is useful to be aware of them, though, since practitioners may be disconcerted by criticism from clients about failures in service or about their behavior. Complaints from clients should always be taken seriously, of course, and a check made to evaluate how much they are justified and action taken accordingly; however, they may also reflect anger or bargaining behavior.

Bereavement and Grief

Many older people are also affected by bereavement and grief. They may have survived longer than friends and their spouses, and many people find the loss of children or other younger family members particularly unfair. The impact of these losses accumulates: for example, the loss of a spouse may bring back the loss many years previously of a parent. Anniversaries of deaths can also be important. While earlier theories of bereavement tended to see it as a series of stages in which people adjust to a loss, or emotional tasks in adjusting to a loss, more recent theory focuses on social expectations and relationships. How people are expected within their culture to respond varies, and there may be specific religious or cultural rituals to be observed. However, in recent years conventional rituals have become less important to many people. Instead, they develop more personal and individualized reactions to the particular personality and life of someone who has died.

Case Example: Shopping in Memory

Joan enjoyed shopping for clothes with family members. Her sister and daughters remembered the anniversary of her death every year by a joint trip to a big town to shop for clothes and have lunch together. This was more important to them than visiting the grave or lighting a candle to her memory. It seemed more personal and appropriate.

Recent sociological ideas are:

- Dual process theory—instead of seeing bereavement as a progression from extensive expressions of grief to greater adjustment to the loss, dual process theory suggests that people switch between different aspects of reaction. The *loss-oriented focus* involves emotional reactions including missing the person who has died, yearning, reminiscing, and reviewing. The *restoration-oriented focus* involves attending to solving practical problems. These include learning new skills to enable the person to construct a new identity to be able to live in the post-loss world (Stroebe & Schut, 1999).
- Continuing bonds theory—instead of adjusting to the loss, people build continuing relationships with the dead person. They arrive at a renewed representation of the person as a part of their life and also reestablish a new social equilibrium, in which the good and bad features of their life with the person are put in the context of their new life, which may include new relationships (Klass, 1996).

- Meaning reconstruction ideas—instead of focusing on loss, these ideas examine how people create an important new meaning and purpose for their lives (Neimeyer, 2001).

Practitioners can help people by enabling them to work positively on their grief, encouraging people to accept these ways of looking at their bereavement, rather than relying on "adjustment" to loss.

Case Example: Completing the Book

Peter had worked with his wife, both history teachers, on a book about the history of their neighborhood, but she did not live to see its completion. Finishing it and seeing it through to press was an important restoration-focused activity for him after her death—it was a fulfilling practical task to complete and meant that he was not always thinking about his loss. He talked to me about it, knowing that I was an experienced author. Among the things he said was that he regretted that his wife had not seen the results of their joint endeavor or worked on the final writing and editing. I took the opportunity to say, "I expect, though, that you heard her telling you about the things that were important to her as you were writing." Saying this, I was trying to make it socially acceptable for him to express a continuing bond, knowing that people often hear or see the person they have lost, but fear that this is unusual or a sign of mental instability. He said that she could not give him her experienced advice, and I said that nevertheless I expected that he could hear just what he knew she would be saying even though she was not present, and that many people had the same experience. He was surprised that I was accepting of such an experience and went on to talk about how he did hear her talking to him.

CONCLUSION

In this chapter, I have brought together a number of issues about social exclusion; these are the practical exclusions that may cut older people off from appropriate help and prevent them from exercising their full citizenship. The chapter covers: ageism and the long-term health and social impact of social inequalities, safeguarding older people when there are emergencies, and finally end-of life and bereavement care. I have suggested in each case that a focus on working with both practical issues and emotional reactions is most effective. Because these are all situations in which older people's social isolation or exclusion may increase, a practitioner can usefully bear in mind the question: how can this older person strengthen their citizenship here?

In this way, these particular issues illustrate the approach of this book to working with older people. A humanistic, citizenship approach centers our practice on the personal and emotional reaction to the often practical issues that older people face in their lives but also on the importance of maintaining older people's social rights and social participation in our society.

FURTHER READING

Working with Vulnerable Adults, by B. Penhale and J. Parker (London: Routledge, 2008).
  This book discusses work with a range of adults who need safeguarding because of social or personal circumstances.
Social Work in End-of-Life and Palliative Care, by M. Reith and M. Payne (Chicago: Lyceum Books, 2009).
  A useful practice handbook coauthored by the present author about practice in end-of-life care, but not focused on working with older people specifically.

Internet Information

Useful Web sites on inequalities are:

Employers' Forum on Age (UK)—http://www.efa.org.uk—good information on aging and work, with an excellent booklet for employers on ageism.
Equity Channel—a useful European Web site on health inequalities: http://www.equitychannel.net.
International Federation on Ageing—http://www.ifa-fiv.org/index.php?option=com_content&view=article&id=421&Itemid=246—useful eight-country survey of age discrimination legislation.
International Policy Centre for Inclusive Growth—good site encouraging concern for social development alongside economic growth, provided by the UN Development Programme: http://www.ipc-undp.org.
Mature project—http://www.mature-project.eu—click on "toolbox" to find documents on age discrimination and employment in many European languages.
PRIAE (Policy Research Institute on Ageing and Ethnicity)—http://www.priae.org/index.htm—contains information and studies about older people in minority ethnic groups in the UK and Europe.
WHO (World Health Organization) Social Determinants of Health Web site—gives access to the Report on the Social Determinants of Health and a wide

range of other material on health inequalities: http://www.who.int/social_determinants/en.

Useful Web sites on elder abuse are as follows:

Action on Elder Abuse (UK)—http://www.elderabuse.org.uk—brief site, with practical rather than academic information.

National Committee for the Prevention of Elder Abuse (U.S.)—http://www.preventelderabuse.org—American association of professionals with an interest in the field, runs the *Journal of Elder Abuse and Neglect*.

National Center on Elder Abuse (U.S.)—http://www.ncea.aoa.gov/NCEAroot/Main_Site/Index.aspx—covers American research and services, good summary of law and research.

Nursing Home Abuse Resource (U.S.)—http://www.nursing-home-abuse-resource.com/index.html—useful information about issues and signs of abuse in care homes; Nursing Home Abuse News may also be useful: http://www.nursinghomeabuse-news.com/index.html.

References

Adams, R., Dominelli, L., & Payne, M. (2009). Towards a critical understanding of social work. In Adams, R., Dominelli, L., & Payne, M. (Eds.), *Social work: Themes, issues, and critical debates* (3rd ed., pp. 1–9). Basingstoke, UK: Palgrave Macmillan.

Addis, S., Davies, M., Greene, G., MacBride-Stewart, S., & Shepherd, M. (2009). The health, social care, and housing needs of lesbian, gay, bisexual, and transgender older people: A review of the literature. *Health & Social Care in the Community, 17*(6), 647–658.

Aldridge, G. (Ed.). (1998). *Music therapy in palliative care: New voices.* London: Jessica Kingsley.

Anti-Ageism Taskforce. (2006). *Ageism in America.* New York: Anti-Ageism Task Force of the International Longevity Center.

Audit Commission. (2004). *Older people—a changing approach: Independence and well-being.* London: Audit Commission. Retrieved July 5, 2010, from http://www.audit-commission.gov.uk/SiteCollectionDocuments/Audit CommissionReports/NationalStudies/OlderPeople1_report.pdf

Audit Commission. (2005). *List of local quality of life indicators* [pull-out section]. London: Audit Commission. Retrieved April 7, 2011, from http://www .audit-commission.gov.uk/SiteCollectionDocuments/AuditCommission Reports/NationalStudies/Pulloutsection.pdf

Audit Commission. (2008). *Don't stop me now: Preparing for an ageing population.* London: Audit Commission. Retrieved July 5, 2010, from http://www .audit-commission.gov.uk/SiteCollectionDocuments/AuditCommission Reports/NationalStudies/DontStopMeNow17July08REP.pdf

Banks, P. (2004). *Policy framework for integrated care for older people: Developed by the Carmen network.* London: King's Fund. Retrieved August 2, 2010, from http://www.ehma.org/files/Policy%20Framework%20for%20Integrated%20 Care%20for%20Older%20People.pdf

Beech, R., & Roberts, D. (2008). *Assistive technology and older people.* London: Social Care Institute for Excellence. Retrieved August 2, 2010, from http:// www.scie.org.uk/publications/briefings/files/briefing28.pdf

Bohlmeijer, E., Smit, F., & Cuijpers, P. (2003). Effects of reminiscence and life review on late-life depression: A meta-analysis. *International Journal of Geriatric Psychiatry, 18*, 1088–1094.

Borrill, C. S., Carletta, J., Carter, C. S., Dawson, J. F., Garrod, S., Rees, A., et al. (2001). *The effectiveness of health care teams in the National Health Service.* Birmingham, UK: University of Aston. Retrieved July 27, 2010, from http://homepages.inf.ed.ac.uk/jeanc/DOH-final-report.pdf

Bradt, J., & Dileo, C. (2010). Music therapy for end-of-life care (review). *Cochrane Database of Systematic Reviews 2010,* Issue 1, Art. no.: CD007169.

Brown Wilson, C. (2009). Developing community in care homes through a relationship-centered approach. *Health & Social Care in the Community, 17*(2), 177–186.

Bullington, J. (2009). Being body: The dignity of human embodiment. In Nordenfelt, L. (Ed.), *Dignity in care for older people* (pp. 54–76). Chichester, UK: Wiley-Blackwell.

Burnside, I., & Haight, B. K. (1992). Reminiscence and life review: Analyzing each concept. *Journal of Advanced Nursing, 17*, 855–862.

Burton, J. (1998). *Managing residential care.* London: Routledge.

Byock, I. (1997). *Dying well: Peace and possibilities at the end of life.* New York: Riverhead.

Bytheway, B. (1995). *Ageism.* Buckingham, UK: Open University Press.

CCETSW. (1975). *Day services: An action plan for training.* London: CCETSW.

Challis, D. (1994). *Care management: Factors influencing its development in the implementation of community care.* London: Department of Health.

Clark, R. L., Burkhauser, R. V., Moon, M., Quinn, J. F., & Smeeding, T. (2004). *The economics of an aging society.* Malden, MA: Blackwell.

Clough, R. (2000). *The practice of residential work.* Basingstoke, UK: Palgrave Macmillan.

Clough, R., Manthorpe, J., Raymond, V., Sumner, K., Bright, L., & Hay, J. (2007). *The support older people want and the services they need.* York, UK: Joseph Rowntree Foundation.

Coleman, P. G. (1986). *Aging and reminiscence processes: Social and clinical implications.* Chichester, UK: Wiley.

Commission of the European Communities. (2009). *Dealing with the impact of an ageing population in the EU (2009 Ageing Report).* Brussels, Belgium: European Commission. Retrieved May 10, 2010, from http://eurlex.europa.eu/Lex UriServ/LexUriServ.do?uri=COM:2009:0180:FIN:EN:PDF

Commission on the Social Determinants of Health. (2008). *Closing the gap in a generation: Health equity through action on the social determinants of health.* Geneva, Switzerland: World Health Organization. Retrieved August 2, 2010, from http://whqlibdoc.who.int/publications/2008/9789241563703_eng.pdf

Cooper, C., Selwood, A., & Livingston, G. (2008). The prevalence of elder abuse and neglect: A systematic review. *Age & Ageing, 37*(2), 151–160.

Crawford, M., Rutter, D., & Thelwall, S. (2003). *User involvement in change management: A review of the literature (Report to the National Co-ordinating Centre for NHS Service Delivery and Organization R & D).* London: NCCSDO. Cited in RIPFA. (2007). *Evidence Cluster: Effective involvement of older people in service planning.* Dartington, UK: Research in Practice for Adults. Retrieved May 6, 2010, from http://www.ripfa.org.uk/images/downloads/evidence_cluster_06.pdf

Cree, V. E., & Davis, A. (2007). *Social work: Voices from the inside.* London: Routledge.

Delivery and Support Team. (2010). *Anticipatory care planning: Frequently asked questions.* Edinburgh, UK: Scottish Government.

Department of Health. (2001). *National service framework for older people.* London: Department of Health. Retrieved July 20, 2010, from http://www.dh.gov.uk/prod_consum_dh/groups/dh_digitalassets/@dh/@en/documents/digital asset/dh_4071283.pdf

Doel, M. (2006). *Using groupwork.* London: Routledge.

Duffin, P. (1992). *Then and now: Reminiscence case studies.* Manchester, UK: Gatehouse.

Egan, M., Wells, J., Byrne, K., Jagiel, S., Stolee, P., Chesworth, B., & Hillier, L. M. (2009). The process of decision-making in home-care case management: Implications for the introduction of universal assessment and information technology. *Health & Social Care in the Community, 17*(4), 371–378.

Erikson, E. R. (1977). *Childhood and society.* London: Paladin.

Estes, C. L., and Associates. (2001). *Social policy and aging: A critical perspective.* Thousand Oaks, CA: Sage.

Evandrou, M. (2000). Social inequalities in later life: The socioeconomic position of older people from ethnic minority groups in Britain. *Population Trends, 101*(Autumn), 11–18. Retrieved July 11, 2010, from http://www.statistics.gov.uk/downloads/theme_population/PT101bookV3.pdf

Evans, G. A., Williams, T. F., Beattie, B. L., Michel, J.-P., & Wilcock, G. K. (2000). *Oxford textbook of geriatric medicine* (2nd ed.). Oxford: Oxford University Press.

Evans, S. (2009). *Community and aging: Maintaining quality of life in housing with care settings*. Bristol, UK: Policy Press.

Eysenbach, G., Powell, P., Englesakis, M., Rizo, C., & Stern, A. (2004). Health-related virtual communities and electronic support groups: Systematic review of the effects of online peer to peer interactions. *British Medical Journal, 328*, 1166. Retrieved August 1, 2010, from http://www.bmj.com/cgi/content/full/328/7449/1166

Fallon, P. (2006). *Elder abuse and/or neglect*. Wellington, UK: Ministry of Social Development. Retrieved July 12, 2010, from http://www.msd.govt.nz/about-msd-and-our-work/publications-resources/literature-reviews/elder-abuse-neglect/index.html

Featherstone, B., & Hepworth, M. (1989). Ageing and old age: Reflections on the postmodern life course. In Bytheway, B., Keil, T., Allott, P., & Bryman, A. (Eds.), *Becoming and being old: Sociological approaches to later life* (pp. 143–157). London: Sage.

Finlay, L. (1993). *Groupwork in occupational therapy*. London: Chapman and Hall.

Fook, J., & Gardner, F. (2007). *Practising critical reflection: A resource handbook*. Maidenhead, UK: Open University Press.

Gallagher, M., & Ireland, E. (2008). *Evaluation of the Nairn anticipatory care project: Final report*. Stirling, UK: University of Stirling Cancer Care Research Centre.

Geldard, K., & Geldard, D. (2005). *Practical counseling skills: An integrative approach*. Basingstoke, UK: Palgrave Macmillan.

Glaser, B. G., & Strauss, A. L. (1965). *Awareness of dying*. New York: Aldine.

Glaser, B. G., & Strauss, A. L. (1968). *Time for dying*. Chicago: Aldine.

Guillemard, A.-M. (2005). The advent of a flexible life course and the reconfigurations of welfare. In Andersen, J. G., Guillemard, A.-M., Kensen, P. H., & Pfau-Effinger, B. (Eds.), *The changing face of welfare: Consequences and outcomes from a citizenship perspective* (pp. 55–73). Bristol, UK: Policy Press.

Hallrup, L. B., Albertsson, D., Bengtsson Tops, A., Dahlberg, K., & Grahn, B. (2009). Elderly women's experiences of living with fall risk in a fragile body: A reflective lifeworld approach. *Health & Social Care in the Community, 17*(4), 379–387.

Hartley, N., & Payne, M. (2008). *The creative arts in palliative care*. London: Jessica Kingsley.

Hayes, J. (with Povey, S.). (2010). *The creative arts in dementia care: Practical person-centered approaches and ideas*. London: Jessica Kingsley.

Henry, C., & Seymour, J. (2008). *Advance care planning: A guide for health and social care staff.* London: Department of Health.

Hodge, D. R. (2000). Spiritual ecomaps: A new diagrammatic tool for assessing marital and family spirituality. *Journal of Marital & Family Therapy, 26*(2), 217–228.

Hodge, D. R., & Williams, T. R. (2002). Assessing African American spirituality with spiritual ecomaps. *Families in Society, 83*(5/6), 285–295.

Holzmann, R., & Hinz, R. (2005). *Old-age income support in the twenty-first century: An international perspective on pension systems and reform.* Washington, DC: World Bank.

Home Office/Department of Health. (2000). *No secrets: Guidance on developing and implementing multi-agency policies and procedures to protect vulnerable adults from abuse.* London: Department of Health. Retrieved August 2, 2010, from http://www.dh.gov.uk/prod_consum_dh/groups/dh_digitalassets/@dh/@en/documents/digitalasset/dh_4074540.pdf

Hong, C. S., Heathcote, J., Quinn, P., & Plummer, M. (2005). The value of reminiscence. *Nursing & Residential Care, 7*(1), 27–29.

Hughes, B. (1995). *Older people and community care: Critical theory and practice.* Buckingham, UK: Open University Press.

Jacobs, P., & Rapoport, J. (2003). *The economics of health and medical care* (5th ed.). Sudbury, MA: Jones and Bartlett.

Janzon, K., & Law, S. (2003). *Older people influencing social care—aspirations and realities* [unpublished paper]. Cited in RIPFA. (2007). *Evidence cluster: Effective involvement of older people in service planning.* Dartington, UK: Research in Practice for Adults. Retrieved May 6, 2010, from http://www.ripfa.org.uk/images/downloads/evidence_cluster_06.pdf

Jones, K. (with Powell, I.). (2008). Situating person and place: Best practice in dementia care. In Jones, K., Cooper, B., & Ferguson, H. (Eds.), *Best practice in social work: Critical perspectives* (pp. 55–70). Basingstoke, UK: Palgrave Macmillan.

Jünger, S., Pestner, M., Eisner, F., Krumm, N., & Radbruch, L. (2007). Criteria for successful multiprofessional cooperation in palliative care teams. *Palliative Medicine, 21*, 347–354.

Just Ageing. (2009a). *Just Ageing? Fairness, equality, and the life course: Final report.* London: Equalities and Human Rights Commission/AgeUK.

Just Ageing. (2009b). *Socioeconomic inequalities in older people's access to and use of public services.* London: Equalities and Human Rights Commission/AgeUK.